T0183450

Lecture Notes in Computer Science   **12439**

Founding Editors

Gerhard Goos
  Karlsruhe Institute of Technology, Karlsruhe, Germany
Juris Hartmanis
  Cornell University, Ithaca, NY, USA

Editorial Board Members

Elisa Bertino
  Purdue University, West Lafayette, IN, USA
Wen Gao
  Peking University, Beijing, China
Bernhard Steffen
  TU Dortmund University, Dortmund, Germany
Gerhard Woeginger
  RWTH Aachen, Aachen, Germany
Moti Yung
  Columbia University, New York, NY, USA

More information about this subseries at http://www.springer.com/series/7412

Jianning Li · Jan Egger (Eds.)

Towards the Automatization of Cranial Implant Design in Cranioplasty

First Challenge, AutoImplant 2020
Held in Conjunction with MICCAI 2020
Lima, Peru, October 8, 2020
Proceedings

 Springer

Editors
Jianning Li (iD)
Graz University of Technology
Graz, Austria

Jan Egger (iD)
Graz University of Technology
Graz, Austria

ISSN 0302-9743 ISSN 1611-3349 (electronic)
Lecture Notes in Computer Science
ISBN 978-3-030-64326-3 ISBN 978-3-030-64327-0 (eBook)
https://doi.org/10.1007/978-3-030-64327-0

LNCS Sublibrary: SL6 – Image Processing, Computer Vision, Pattern Recognition, and Graphics

© Springer Nature Switzerland AG 2020
This work is subject to copyright. All rights are reserved by the Publisher, whether the whole or part of the material is concerned, specifically the rights of translation, reprinting, reuse of illustrations, recitation, broadcasting, reproduction on microfilms or in any other physical way, and transmission or information storage and retrieval, electronic adaptation, computer software, or by similar or dissimilar methodology now known or hereafter developed.
The use of general descriptive names, registered names, trademarks, service marks, etc. in this publication does not imply, even in the absence of a specific statement, that such names are exempt from the relevant protective laws and regulations and therefore free for general use.
The publisher, the authors and the editors are safe to assume that the advice and information in this book are believed to be true and accurate at the date of publication. Neither the publisher nor the authors or the editors give a warranty, expressed or implied, with respect to the material contained herein or for any errors or omissions that may have been made. The publisher remains neutral with regard to jurisdictional claims in published maps and institutional affiliations.

This Springer imprint is published by the registered company Springer Nature Switzerland AG
The registered company address is: Gewerbestrasse 11, 6330 Cham, Switzerland

Preface

The AutoImplant Cranial Implant Design Challenge (AutoImplant 2020: https://autoimplant.grand-challenge.org/) was initialized jointly by the Graz University of Technology (TU Graz) and the Medical University of Graz (MedUni Graz), Austria, through an interdisciplinary project "Clinical Additive Manufacturing for Medical Applications" (CAMed: https://www.medunigraz.at/camed/) between the two institutions. The project aims to provide more affordable, faster, and patient-friendly solutions to the design and manufacturing of medical implants, including cranial implants, which is needed in order to repair a defective skull from a brain tumor surgery or trauma.

In most of the current clinical practices, cranial implants are designed and manufactured externally of the hospitals, and the design process requires commercial software and professional designers. Thus, the procedure remains to be time-consuming, expensive, and patient-unfriendly (in the worst-case scenario, the patient has to come back to the hospital several times, getting repeatedly anesthetized, until a fitting implant is designed, manufactured, and implanted).

Recent years have witnessed an increase in computer-aided design (CAD) of cranial implants, which exploits free, open-source, and easy-to-use software. However, these CAD approaches still cannot fit in with an 'in operation room (in-OR)' cranial implant manufacturing pipeline, as they are not fast enough and require heavy human interactions.

In order to tackle the aforementioned problem, the First AutoImplant Cranial Implant Design Challenge (AICIDC) was held as a satellite event at the Medical Image Computing and Computer Assisted Interventions (MICCAI 2020) conference in Lima, Peru, (held virtually due to COVID-19), with the aim to attract worldwide solutions for a fast and fully automatic cranial implant design. To date (beginning of October, 2020), the challenge attracted 150 registered users from all over the world (please see the world map at the end of the preface) who obtained access to the challenge dataset. The participants come from different backgrounds, like academia and industry. In the design of the challenge, cranial implant design was being technically formulated as a 3D volumetric shape learning problem, as the skull itself can be viewed as a two dimensional manifold embedded in a three dimensional volumetric space (of a computed tomography scan). The implication behind such formulation is twofold. First, if a complete skull can be predicted given a corrupted skull, the cranial implant can be obtained by simply taking the difference between the two skulls (shape completion). Second, from the perspective of shape learning, it is also possible to predict directly the missing portion i.e., the implant from a corrupted skull.

Such a problem formulation also opens the possibility of solving the medical problem with a much broader methodology, such as deep learning, statistical shape model (SSM), and therefore a fully automated cranial implant design pipeline can be envisaged.

It is a well-known characteristic that learning-based solutions are built upon large quantities of labeled data. However, the real defective skulls from a brain tumor surgery or trauma are difficult to obtain, due to both the rarity of related operations and the requirement of the approval from the institutional review board (IRB). We solve this issue by 'faking' defects on normal/healthy skulls, as head CT scans are required in many clinical routines and thus it is possible to collect them in larger quantity.

The challenge dataset was adapted from the public head CT collection CQ500 (http://headctstudy.qure.ai/dataset). We selected over 200 healthy skulls and on each of them a virtual defect is injected. The resultant defective skulls serve as the input while the original healthy skulls or the removed bony structure serve as the ground truth (100 for training and 100 for testing). The virtual defects are simplified compared to those from craniotomy and trauma, which tend to have greater irregularity. An additional test set containing 10 skulls with distinct defect shapes, sizes, and positions, from those in the training and test set has been additionally created. These cases are used to evaluate how well the algorithms generalize to varied defects – a characteristic highly desired in clinical practice as the defects from craniotomy also vary depending on the intracranial pathology to be operated on for each particular patient. (note, we also have a data article in submission about our collection, which has taken longer than expected to get published. However, to make the proceedings complete we also provided a data description at the beginning of these proceedings). Having a uniform collection of datasets for a challenge has the advantage to also have a uniform and objective evaluation for the submitted results of the various algorithmic approaches. A drawback is, however, that this course of action does not provide a quantitative evaluation for further cases 'outside' the challenge dataset pool. At the very most, the challenge results can be see as proof of concept that provides an indication for the general field as a whole. It would also not be feasible to cover all medical centers with their specific scanners and scanner protocols in a single challenge or research work. Nonetheless, to increase the variety slightly, we included one work within these proceedings that uses a data collection that is completely independent from the official challenge datasets, which shows and proves a principle translation of our challenge goal to other medical image acquisitions. In future organizations of the challenge, we plan to provide real clinical craniotomy skulls as the final pool of evaluation. In addition, we are working on a second collection of skulls, which will allow a multi-center evaluation of algorithms.

We released the whole training set to the registered participants. However, for the test set, only the defective skulls are released. The ground truth skulls and implants are kept by the organizers. For evaluation, participants submit the predicted implants to the organizer and a .csv file containing the scores, Dice Similarity Score (DSC) and Hausdorff distance (HD), and each of the test cases are returned to them. The final ranking is obtained by taking the average of the DSC ranking (in descending order) and the HD ranking (in ascending order).

Until the submission deadline (September 14, 2020), 10 manuscripts were received and 9 of them received an early acceptance after double-blind reviews. One got accepted after rigorous revision and rebuttal based on the reviewers' comments. Each paper was assigned three to four reviewers. The camera-ready version of these papers are 8–12 pages long. Of the 10 accepted solutions, 6 of them are able to make accurate predictions on all the 110 test cases, while the other 4 fail on the additional 10 test cases. The accepted solutions cover a wide spectrum of methodologies such as statistical shape models, generative adversarial networks, and auto-encoder style neural networks. In these papers, two essential problems were addressed: 1) How to efficiently tackle high dimensional data in deep learning; and 2) How to improve the generalization performance of deep learning models through the use of shape priors, regularization, and data augmentation. The generalization performance in our challenge mainly refers to the ability to generalize to varied skull defects. These solutions can therefore serve as a good benchmark for future publications regarding 3D volumetric shape learning and cranial implant design.

Finally, to enable the easy-accessibility of automatic cranial implant design solutions to non-technical users, we implemented a web-based platform – StudierFenster (http://studierfenster.at/ or http://studierfenster.icg.tugraz.at/), where these solutions can be integrated. As an example, one of our previous automatic cranial implant design solutions (deep learning-based) was implemented in StudierFenster and can be accessed via a web browser. Please stay healthy!

Statistics

Number of users: 150

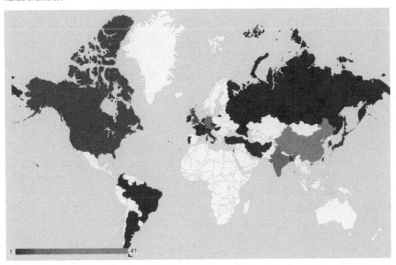

World Map: Snapshot of the AutoImplant challenge as of the beginning of October 2020, showing the overall number of registered participants and the geographic distribution around the world.

October 2020   Jianning Li
                                                                            Jan Egger

Organization

General Chairs

Jianning Li   Graz University of Technology, Austria
Jan Egger   Graz University of Technology and Medical University
                                 of Graz, Austria

Program Committee

Victor Alves   University of Minho, Portugal
Xiaojun Chen   Shanghai Jiao Tong University, China
Christina Gsaxner   Graz University of Technology, Austria
Oldřich Kodym   Brno University of Technology, Czech Republic
Marcell Krall   Medical University of Graz, Austria
Antonio Pepe   Graz University of Technology, Austria
Karin Pistracher   Medical University of Graz, Austria
Ute Schäfer   Medical University of Graz, Austria
Dieter Schmalstieg   Graz University of Technology, Austria
Michal Spanel   Brno University of Technology, Czech Republic
Gord von Campe   Medical University of Graz, Austria
Ulrike Zefferer   Medical University of Graz, Austria

Sponsors

Acknowledgements

The challenge received the support of CAMed – Clinical additive manufacturing for medical applications (COMET K-Project 871132), which is funded by the Austrian Federal Ministry of Transport, Innovation and Technology (BMVIT), the Austrian Federal Ministry for Digital and Economic Affairs (BMDW), and the Styrian Business Promotion Agency (SFG). Furthermore, the challenge sees the support of the Austrian Science Fund (FWF) KLI 678-B31: "enFaced: Virtual and Augmented Reality Training and Navigation Module for 3D-Printed Facial Defect Reconstructions" and the TU Graz Lead Project (Mechanics, Modeling and Simulation of Aortic Dissection). We also want to thank the Computer Algorithms for Medicine Laboratory (https://cafe-lab.org/) members and the paper reviewers. Finally, we thank Zhaodi Deng for the design of the challenge logo.

Contents

Patient Specific Implants (PSI)

Cranioplasty in the Neurosurgical Clinical Routine

Gord von Campe[✉] and Karin Pistracher

Department of Neurosurgery, Medical University of Graz, Auenbruggerplatz 29, 8036 Graz,
Austria
gord.von-campe@medunigraz.at

Abstract. Implants are an important instrument in modern medicine for providing
patients with a higher quality of life after accident- or disease-related functional
limitations. In cranial neurosurgery, reconstructive implants are primarily used to
restore normal skull function and anatomical integrity after severe head trauma,
resection of bone affecting tumors, or bone loss due to infection or spontaneous
postoperative bone flap resorption. Patient specific implants (PSI) are custom-
made implants manufactured to each patient's individual anatomical specifications, and the advent of new manufacturing techniques and materials opens the
opportunity for a closer integration into the clinical routine. The following contri-
bution aims at giving non-medical participants of the AutoImplant challenge some
insight into the neurosurgical perspective on when cranial implants are needed,
what the surgical procedures are, what cranioplasty methods currently are available, what criteria should be met by the implants, and where the limitations of the
current manufacturing solutions lie.

Keywords: Neurosurgery · Cranioplasty · Patient specific implant · 3D printing

1 Patient Specific Implants (PSI) in Cranial Neurosurgery

1.1 Primary Indications for Cranioplasty in Neurosurgery

Cranial bone defects are the result of a number of traumatic and pathological processes
and can occur anywhere in the skull.

In severe head injuries with complex comminuted fractures, a reconstruction of the
multiple, in the case of open injuries even sometimes contaminated bone fragments is
not always practicable or advisable, so that their surgical removal will result in a loss
of cranial bone. Although a decompressive craniectomy might initially be indicated to
allow for brain recovery from brain swelling, ultimate covering of the bony defect will
be required.

Various benign and malignant neoplastic diseases can either remodel or destruct
the skull bone structures. Meningiomas are intracranial, mostly benign tumors arising
from the arachnoidal cells of the meninges (membranous layers surrounding the brain).
They can cause osteocondensation of the adjoining bone, which, in extreme cases, will
cause a deformation of the skull visible from the outside. The anaplastic (malignant)

© Springer Nature Switzerland AG 2020
J. Li and J. Egger (Eds.): AutoImplant 2020, LNCS 12439, pp. 1–9, 2020.
https://doi.org/10.1007/978-3-030-64327-0_1

variants can have a highly aggressive, infiltrative and osteodestructive growth pattern. Other examples of skull bone involving tumors include Langerhans cell histiocytosis (histiocytosis X), haemangiomas, cavernous angiomas (see Fig. 1), benign (osteomas, fibrous dysplasias) or malignant (osteosarcomas) primary bone tumors and secondary metastatic tumors (carcinomas). Surgical treatment or diagnostic procedures of these tumors will generally result in a more or less extensive bony defect that will require appropriate covering or filling.

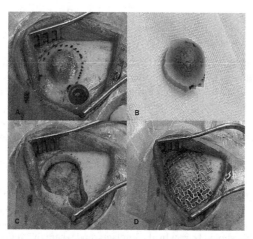

Fig. 1. Cavernous angioma of the left frontal bone causing visible and palpable bone deformity under the skin. (A) Surgical removal is achieved by placing a small burr hole near the lesion, which is then drilled out using a vertical craniotome (milling cutter). (B) Removed lesion with healthy bone margins. (C) Resulting skull bone defect with intact underlying meningeal layer. (D) Non-PSI covering of the defect with a small titanium mesh.

Spontaneous resorption of reimplanted bone flaps after a neurosurgical procedure is a well-recognized complication in children, but also occurs more frequently than initially suspected in the adult population [1]. Resulting loosening and shrinking of the bone flap with pain symptoms, visible deformation (skin retraction) and wound healing complications frequently require a secondary surgical intervention to correct the defect.

Primary and secondary (postoperative) bone infections also account for a number of skull bone defects. Surgical treatment of an intracranial empyema might make the reimplantation of the adjoining bone flap less than desirable, and postoperative bone flap infections usually require the permanent removal of the affected bone flap. After appropriate antibiotic treatment, the resulting bone defect will entail delayed covering.

1.2 Patient Specific Implants (PSI)

Regardless of the primary origin of the neurocranial skull bone defect, it might lead to functional and physical complaints if left uncovered. Also, given the important role that the head in general plays in the individual uniqueness, additional emotional and body schema integrity disturbances will ultimately negatively impact the patient's quality of life. Various methods and techniques are currently available to substitute for the bone loss: their common goal is to restore the mechanical function, reinstate the protective role (brain) and reestablish a normal anatomical state.

"Generic" implants generally consist of either (mostly) autologous bone grafts (e.g. split calvarial, rib), bone cement (e.g. Palacos®), or malleable metallic (titanium) meshes (see Fig. 1D and 2). These methods mainly restore the mechanical and protective functions. Aesthetic results can be somewhat improved by using prefabricated molds based on the patient's anatomy to appropriately shape the cement [2] or mesh [3]. The main advantages are a high intraoperative availability and a relatively low cost. However, aesthetic results can be suboptimal and anatomical structures are only partially restored [4].

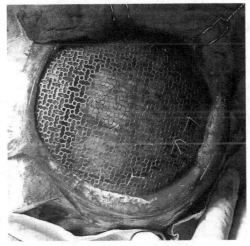

Fig. 2. Non-PSI solution using a titanium mesh to cover a large skull bone defect. Tack-up sutures can be seen to reduce the void between the mesh and the underlying meningeal layer (as opposed to a PSI which would fill the defect, reestablishing the thickness and contour of the missing bone).

Patient specific implants (PSI) on the other hand are custom-made implants based exactly on each and every individual patient's anatomical bony structures and relationships as inferred from high resolution computer tomographic reconstructions (see Fig. 3). Several materials and manufacturing techniques (milling, 3D printing) are commercially available: PEEK (polyether ether ketone, e.g. Stryker, Synthes, Xilloc Medical, 3di, KLS Martin Group), titanium (e.g. 3di, Ortho Baltic Implants, KLS Martin Group), bioceramics (e.g. 3di), and calcium phosphate composite (e.g. OssDsign), to name only a few. In addition to restoring the mechanical and protective functions, these custom-fit implants also achieve a perfect cosmetic repair. There is however a higher cost involved, and, due to the out-of-clinic production, this solution is generally not available immediately (intraoperatively). Also, additional imaging and exposure to ionizing radiation will be required, as modelling is based on computed tomography (CT).

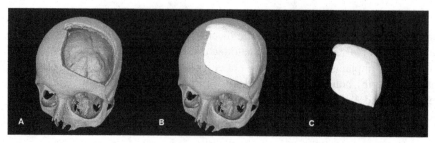

Fig. 3. Creative process of a PSI. (A) High resolution 3D reconstruction of the patient's skull, based on high resolution CT scan images after segmentation, showing the bony defect to be filled. (B) Implant modelling to restore function and normal anatomical relationships. (C) Resulting computerized implant model ready for manufacturing.

2   Clinical Workflow

2.1   Current Clinical Workflow

Generally speaking, and regardless of the reason that led to the skull defect, the use of a PSI entails several steps as outlined in Fig. 4: a primary surgery, an appropriately timed high resolution CT scan, an external design and manufacturing process, and finally a delayed second surgery for the implantation of the PSI.

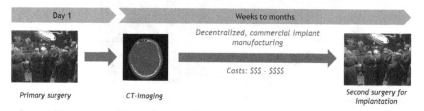

Fig. 4. Summary of the current clinical workflow when a PSI is used.

In severe traumatic head injury with complex comminuted fractures, primary surgery consists of removal of the bone fragments and - depending on the absence or presence of brain swelling - covering or not of the resulting skull defect. Since primary surgery is always performed in an emergency setting, concomitant implantations of a PSI is never possible, and immediate covering, if clinically appropriate, is often done using metallic meshes, since these are readily available. If the use of a PSI is indicated (mostly based on size and location of the defect), its implantation will require a second surgery after recovery from the initial traumatic brain injuries.

Tumorous skull involvement with bony remodeling or destruction warrants excision of the altered bone, allowing for a healthy margin. Although mostly not done as an emergency procedure, the preoperative determination of the exact extent of the bone resection is not always possible solely based on diagnostic imaging, since tumor infiltration might go beyond the radiologically visible borders; in most cases it is therefore not feasible to design and obtain a PSI before the primary surgery has taken place. Furthermore, a perfect fit of a prefabricated PSI would require a precise navigational-guided bone resection, which is not always practicable. In most cases therefore a decision has to be made, again based on location and size of the resulting defect, whether to use a mesh for immediate/temporary covering, or a PSI which will require a second operation.

Although metallic meshes can and have been used for concomitant covering of a skull defect resulting from the removal of an infected postoperative bone flap, immediate availability of a PSI in this situation is not of high priority, as its implantation is usually postponed to after completion of an appropriate antibiotic therapy course, which generally takes several weeks anyhow.

Except in the setting of infectious bone involvements, where the bony structures are rarely completely destroyed or majorly remodeled, normal anatomy might not be known prior to surgery. Head trauma often involves younger adults, without prior "normal" imaging, and in tumor cases diagnostic imaging shows the already altered bone. Only if the patient had some imaging done for other reasons before the traumatic or pathological process occurred or was known, could these images potentially be used as a "template" for the implant design. However, even if available, prior imaging is rarely of sufficiently high resolution to be usable for adequate 3D reconstructions.

2.2 Possible Future Workflow

Obvious shortcomings of the current clinical workflow are:

1) *Timing*: As the use of pre-designed implants is quite coercive and surgically not very practicable, PSIs are generally not readily available at the time of the first surgery. Also, since natural remodeling of the skull defect does occur over time, high resolution CT imaging and implant manufacturing have to be carefully timed to ensure a perfect fit (only plastic polymer implants can be reworked intraoperatively if needed).
2) *Costs*: Although they perfectly fulfill all requirements (mechanical, functional and cosmetic) for an ideal reconstruction of various skull defects, PSIs are usually much more expensive than the "generic" solutions. Depending on size and/or location of the defect, the latter are therefore frequently used instead of PSIs for economic reasons.
3) *CT imaging*: Current implant design strategies rely on a 3D skull/defect model obtained by segmentation of a high resolution CT scan. This requires specific imaging protocols defined by the manufacturers and exposes the patient to additional ionizing radiations (1.5–2.3 mSv vs. around 1.2 mSv for a conventional diagnostic CT scan).

Access to an onsite manufacturing facility could greatly improve implant availability by reducing image transfer times and allowing for rapid imaging protocol error corrections, by decreasing production times, and by tightly integrating with the planning of the surgical procedure. Cost reduction could be achieved through the use of more economical polymers and manufacturing procedures (e.g. block milling vs. filament printing), making PSIs accessible to all patients, regardless of insurance coverage, defect size or defect location. A possible in-house workflow using a cost-effective medical 3D printer is outlined in Fig. 5, but also introduces new challenges yet to be overcome.

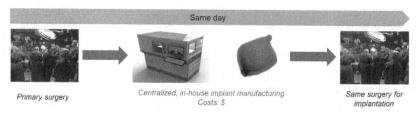

Fig. 5. Possible clinical workflow using an in-house 3D implant design and printing solution.

3   Cranial Implant Generation Challenges

3.1   Imaging and Anatomy

PSIs are custom-made to perfectly fit individual anatomical specifications and features. Their design requires an anatomical model of the patient's skull and bone defect as a common ground (see Fig. 3A). Currently, this model is generated by extracting the bony skull structures from a high resolution CT scan (see Fig. 6).

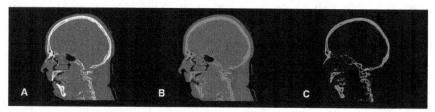

Fig. 6. Segmentation procedure. Starting point are high resolution CT scan images (A). Using thresholding or higher-level methods, the bony skull structures (in green) are isolated from the surrounding soft tissue (B), resulting in a high resolution mask layer (C). A 3D model of the skull (see Fig. 3A) can then be created by combining multiple high resolution mask layers from the same high resolution CT scan into a volume.

Segmentation can be time-consuming and necessitates specific software and appropriate knowledge. Automatic segmentation can be difficult, since bone density can vary by age, gender and anatomical location. Furthermore high resolution CT imaging exposes the patient to non-negligible amounts of additional ionizing radiations. Intraoperative implant generation would require intraoperative CT imaging, which is commonly not available. To address some of these limitations, a light-weight hand-held laser scanner could be used: easy to operate and handle, fast in generating 3D models (of the skull defect), its contactless mode of operation is ideally suited for the sterile environment of an operating room.

3.2 Implant Model Design

PSI manufacturing always requires a 3D model of the implant to be produced. The proper filling of the skull defect is mostly done manually and requires adequate anatomical knowledge: in most cases normal (i.e. premorbid) anatomy is not known, and mirroring is only of limited use since skulls are rarely perfectly symmetric (or the defect is over the midline, thus affecting both sides at the same time). The removed bone flap can only be used as a template if the underlying pathological process is neither bone remodeling nor bone destructing. A desirable approach could be a fast (semi-)automatic implant design using deep learning algorithms trained on a large structured database of segmented skull CT scans (allowing for variations in age, gender, etc.).

3.3 Implant Manufacturing

Total implant generation time is the sum of segmentation time, model design time, manufacturing time and sterilization time. If a custom implant is to be made available at the end of the primary surgery, manufacturing will require a reasonable fast process, which can be either subtractive or generative.

In subtractive processes, 3D models are milled from a block of material in computer-controlled CNC (Computer Numerical Control) milling machines [5]. This method is mainly used for titanium or PEEK implants [6].

In generative processes, material is added layer by layer in a computer-controlled manner. These so called 3D printing processes are particularly suitable for polymers and allow for geometrically much more complex shapes to be generated from the digital data than milling. Well established processes include stereolithography (SLA) for photoactive synthetic resins, selective laser sintering (SLS) for metal or plastic powders, and fused deposition modeling (FDM) for thermoplastics. Limiting factors include machine speed and time required for the material cool down and/or polymerization.

4 Requirements for Cranial Implants

Due to the value and complexity of the underlying anatomical structures (brain), cranial PSIs have to fulfill several requirements:

1) *Mechanical properties*: Ideally, weight, resistance and stiffness of the implant should be identical to the missing skull bone it replaces. This implies adequate power absorption and dissipation in cases of a light trauma, and ultimate controlled breakage ("crumple zone") in a major trauma to prevent or minimize direct brain injury by the implant itself.
2) *Biocompatibility*: Chemical interaction with or compound diffusion into the surrounding bone and soft tissue (meninges, muscles, skin) needs to be nonexistent or minimal, since toxic or heavy inflammatory reactions can lead to increased morbidity (painful swelling), delayed wound healing or even implant rejection.
3) *Thermostability*: Adequate brain insulation from cold and sufficient protection from excessive heat require an implant material with low thermal conductivity. It also has to be able to sustain higher temperatures without deformation for proper washing and sterilization prior to implantation.

4) *"Implantability"*: The free borders of the skull defect might exhibit slow regenerative changes between the time the implant was produced and is finally implanted, which might lead to misfitting. The implant material should therefore allow for small size or shape adjustments using standard intraoperative burrs and tools. Ordinary bone flap fixation methods (sutures, clamps, micro plates and screws) should also be applicable to PSIs, ideally with freely selectable fixation points.

5) *Diagnostic compatibility*: As either the underlying pathology that caused the skull defect (e.g. tumor) or future diseases might require further CT or magnetic resonance imaging, the properties of the compound used for the implant should cause no or only minimal radiological artifacts.

Although a large number of new alloplastic materials for orthopedic and craniofacial surgery have been developed in the past [7], most commercially available implants are currently made from metal (titanium) or biocompatible plastic polymers (PEEK, poly(methyl methacrylate)(PMMA)). Metal implants have a high thermal conductivity, resulting in unpleasant sensations for the patient at both low and high temperatures in the case of cranial implants. Evaluation of postoperative or follow-up radiological images is made difficult by the metal-associated artifacts, which can also negatively impact possibly needed radiation-based treatments. Finally, metal implants cannot be easily reworked intraoperatively in the event of fitting inaccuracies. Polymer implants, on the other hand, have a low thermal conductivity, high radiolucency, do not interfere with radiation therapy, are easily reworkable intraoperatively, and compare favorably with bone in their biomechanical properties. In cranial implants PEEK has emerged as an industry standard fulfilling all these requirements with a very low complication rate.

5   Conclusion and Outlook

Cranial reconstructive procedures might be required immediately, i.e. at the end of the primary surgery, or implemented later in a second surgery. Currently, immediate non-PSI cranioplasty is mainly achieved using malleable metallic meshes or manual modelling of bone cement (e.g. Palacos®). The latter method allows for more flexibility, but requires sculpturing skills; cement polymerization is a highly exothermic reaction, and the acrylic material can trigger a marked local inflammatory reaction. Although these approaches are cost-effective and usually acceptable for small defects, they can lead to suboptimal biomechanical and cosmetic results in cases of larger defects.

An in-house PSI design and manufacturing process might obviate the necessity for a delayed second surgical procedure, potentially lessening complications and reducing overall hospital costs. Time however represents a major challenge, since implant design, manufacturing and sterilization have all to be accomplished within the non-extensible timeframe of the primary surgery.

Implant manufacturing always requires a computerized 3D model, but 3D modelling is not a primary medical or surgical skill: appropriate 3D artist or CAD abilities are required, and, depending on the size and complexity of the implant, its design can be time-consuming. Current developments in deep learning algorithms might (semi-)automate this task, bringing us one step closer to a "virtual warehouse" of readily available, but custom-fit, patient specific implants.

Fast 3D printing hardware is already available, but manufacturing speed is mainly dictated by the physicochemical properties of the applied material: only medically approved polymers (e.g. PEEK) can be used for PSIs, and their heating, cooling and polymerization times are given constants. However, the design of new biocompatible high-performance polymers with different properties might open the way for faster implant manufacturing processes. This will require further close cooperation between clinicians, engineers, materials scientists, computer scientists and basic researchers.

References

1. Stieglitz, L.H., Fung, C., Murek, M., Fichtner, J., Raabe, A., Beck, J.: What happens to the bone flap? Long-term outcome after reimplantation of cryoconserved bone flaps in a consecutive series of 92 patients. Acta Neurochir. **157**(2), 275–280 (2014). https://doi.org/10.1007/s00701-014-2310-7
2. Marbacher, S., et al.: Intraoperative template-molded bone flap reconstruction for patient-specific cranioplasty. Neurosurg. Rev. **35**, 527–535 (2012)
3. Sunderland, I.R.P., Edwards, G., Mainprize, J., Antonyshyn, O.: A technique for intraoperative creation of patient-specific titanium mesh implants. Plast. Surg. (Oakv) **23**(2), 95–99 (2015)
4. Kriegel, R.J., Schaller, C., Clusmann, H.: Cranioplasty for large skull defects with PMMA (Polymethylmethacrylate) or Tutoplast processed autogenic bone grafts. Zentralbl. Neurochir. **68**, 182–189 (2007)
5. Rüegg, A., Gygax, P.: A generalized kinematics model for three- to five-axis milling machines and their implementation in a CNC. CIRP Ann. – Manufact. Technol. **41**, 547–550 (1992)
6. Wintermantel, E.: Medizintechnik: Life Science Engineering - Interdisziplinarität, Biokompatibilität, Technologien, Implantate, Diagnostik, Werkstoffe, Zertifizierung, Business, 5th edn. Springer, Berlin (2009)
7. Sinn, D.P., Bedrossian, E., Vest, A.K.: Craniofacial implant surgery. Oral Maxillofac. Surg. Clin. North Am. **23**(321–335), vi–vii (2011)

Dataset Descriptor for the AutoImplant Cranial Implant Design Challenge

Jianning Li[1,2(✉)] and Jan Egger[1,2,3]

[1] Institute of Computer Graphics and Vision, Graz University of Technology,
Graz, Austria
{jianning.li,egger}@icg.tugraz.at
[2] Computer Algorithms for Medicine Laboratory (Café-Lab), Graz, Austria
[3] Department of Oral and Maxillofacial Surgery, Medical University of Graz,
Graz, Austria

Abstract. This data descriptor elaborates on a dataset that can be used for the development of automatic, data-driven approaches for cranial implant design, which is a challenging task in cranioplasty. The dataset includes 210 complete skulls as well as their corresponding defective skulls and the implants, resulting in a total of $210 \times 3 = 630$ files in NRRD format. We split the dataset into a training set and a test set, each containing 100 and 110 completes skulls as well as the associated defective skulls and implants, respectively. The complete skulls are segmented from the public head computed tomography (CT) collection *CQ500* (http://headctstudy.qure.ai/dataset), which is licensed under *CC BY-NC-SA 4.0*, using thresholding (Hounsfield units ≥ 150). On each complete skull, a synthetic defect, which resembles a real defect from craniotomy, is injected. In the test set, 100 skulls have similar defects to the training set, with respect to defect size, shape and position, while the last 10 skulls have distinct defects. The whole training set and the defective skulls in the test set are released to the participants of the MIC-CAI 2020 AutoImplant Challenge (https://autoimplant.grand-challenge.org/). The ground truth of the test set, i.e., the complete skulls and the implants are kept private by the organizers for a single blind an objective evaluation of the participant's results.

Keywords: AutoImplant dataset · Descriptor · Deep learning · Cranial implant design

1 Data Origin and Selection Criteria

The challenge dataset is adapted from a public head computed tomography (CT) collection CQ500 (http://headctstudy.qure.ai/dataset), which is licensed under *CC BY-NC-SA 4.0*. In consultation with our medical partners, we selected 200 unique skulls from the collection based on the criteria that the skulls should

---

https://autoimplant.grand-challenge.org/.

© Springer Nature Switzerland AG 2020
J. Li and J. Egger (Eds.): AutoImplant 2020, LNCS 12439, pp. 10–15, 2020.
https://doi.org/10.1007/978-3-030-64327-0_2

be complete (without evident damage and deformity of the cranial bone) and the images are of high-quality (slice thickness less than 1 mm). In case a Digital Imaging and Communications in Medicine (DICOM) file contains multiple series/studies, only the study with the highest number of slices have been selected. The volumetric dimension of the skulls is $512 \times 512 \times Z$, where Z is the number of axial slices. The original head CT is in the format of DICOM and each selected DICOM file is converted to a single nearly raw raster data (NRRD) file for easier handling and further processing within the challenge.

2   Skull Processing

The overall workflow of converting the raw NRRD files to the challenge dataset is shown in Fig. 1. The workflow contains three major operations: skull segmentation, denoising, and defect injection. Each operation is explained below.

Fig. 1. Dataset creation workflow (from left to right): The head computed tomography (CT) scan, skull segmentation using thresholding, CT head holder removal, artificial defect injection and the implant (i.e., the removed part from the skull).

2.1   Skull Segmentation

The skull bone was segmented from each head CT using a fixed threshold. The lower threshold is chosen empirically to be 150 Hounsfield Units (HU) for all skulls and the upper threshold is the maximum density of each CT scan. The operation results in binary voxel grid (also in NRRD format) containing the complete bony surface of the skulls.

2.2   Denoising

As the head holder of the CT machine has also high density in CT images, the aforementioned thresholding operation will also preserve the head holders, which are irrelevant components for the cranial implant design task. Thus, we removed the head holders from the binary files automatically using a 3D connected component analysis, given that the skulls are the largest component.

2.3   Defect Injection

An artificial defect was injected into each of the 200 complete skulls. The artificial defects resemble real defects from craniotomy (e.g., brain tumor surgery),
according to a craniotomy dataset [1]. Figure 2 (right) shows a defective skull
from craniotomy and the corresponding cranial implant designed by experts. We
can see a small roundish drilling hole in one corner of the defect, which is caused
by a craniotome. The craniotome is a tool used by neurosurgeons to open the
skull of the patient. The artificial defect, as can be seen from Fig. 2 (left), also
has such roundish corners. The dataset is then split into a training set containing 100 complete skulls and the associated defective skulls, and the implant, and
the remaining skulls form the test set, which is referred to as test set (100). The
defects in the training set and test set (100) are similar in terms of the position
and shape, as shown in Fig. 2 (left). However, considering that in craniotomy,
the shape and position of the defect can be different for different patients based
on their individual conditions, e.g. the location of the brain tumor, we created
test set (10), which has varied defects, as can be seen in Fig. 2 (middle). The
test set (10) are created by randomly selecting 10 complete skulls from test set
(100) and injecting varied defects into the selected skulls.

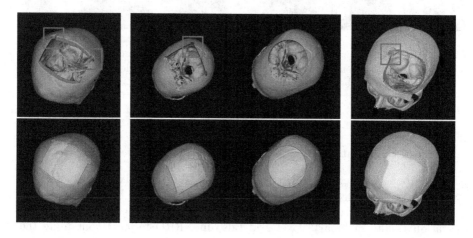

Fig. 2. From left to right: The artificial defect used in the training set and test set
(100), the defects used in test set (10) and an illustration of a real skull defect from
craniotomy. The second row shows the corresponding 'implanted' skulls. The implants
are shown in yellow. The rightmost implant for the real case has been manually designed
by an expert. (Color figure online)

3   Quantitative Dataset Parameters

In this section, we show the quantitative parameters of the challenge dataset.
Table 1 shows the maximum (top), minimum (middle) and average number (bottom) of axial slices ($n-slice$) as well as the voxel occupancy rate (VOR) of

the training set, test set (100) and test set (10). The **VOR** is defined as the percentage of occupied voxels in the whole image volume:

$$\mathbf{VOR} = \frac{\sum \mathbf{V}}{N} \tag{1}$$

where $\sum \mathbf{V}$ represents the number of occupied voxels the image volume $\mathbf{V}$ and $N = 512 \times 512 \times Z$ is the total number of voxel grids in the volume. The distribution of these parameters is given in Fig. 3. We can see that the maximum **VOR** for the complete skull is no greater than 10%. It shows that, unlike other medical images, which are usually dense, the images in our dataset are of sparse nature, i.e., the skulls are hollow and the skull surfaces are distributed sparsely across the image volumes. Another characteristic is that the skull data is binary, containing only 1 (voxel belonging to the skull surface) and 0 (background).

Table 1. Statistics of the challenge dataset.

	Training set	Test set (100)	Test set (10)
n − slice	394	331	288
	211	151	218
	255.7	254.24	240.1
skull VOR (%)	9.81	9.15	7.79
	3.64	3.73	4.79
	5.99	5.96	5.79

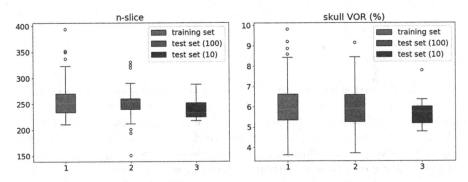

Fig. 3. Boxplot of the **n − slice** and **VOR** in the training set, test set (100) and test set (10).

Another important parameter of the dataset is the defect variation, which is represented by the position and size of the bounding box of the defect. The bounding box is a rectangular box that tightly encloses the defected region on the skull. The defect variation comes from two aspects: position variation, which can be defined as the starting point coordinates (x, y, z) of the bounding box and size variation, which can be defined as the size of the bounding box in x-, y- and z-direction in the $512 \times 512 \times Z$ volume. Figure 4 shows the position (first row) and size (second row) variation of the training set, test set (100) and test set (10). The shape variation of the defect comes mainly from the skull itself, as each individual skull has a unique shape.

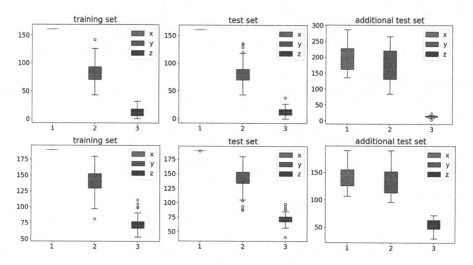

Fig. 4. Defect variations for the training set, the regular 100 test cases (middle) and the additional 10 test cases (right). First row: position variation. Second row: size variation.

4   Conclusion

The aforementioned skull data can be used for two other purposes, in addition to serving as the challenge dataset [2]. First, to develop automated, data-driven solutions for cranial implant design [3,4]. In clinical practice, the cranial implant is designed by experts according to a defective skull using commercial software. Second, to serve as a benchmark for volumetric shape learning tasks such as volumetric shape completion. Currently, most shape completion related papers, such as A. Dai et al. [5] and X. Han et al. [6], use ShapeNet [7] as a benchmark. ShapeNet contains various objects such as chairs, cars and airplanes in 3D point clouds representation. To use the dataset for shape completion, the point clouds needs to be voxelized and the resulting voxel girds are of low dimension e.g., 32^3. In contrast, the skulls in our dataset are high dimensional ($512 \times 512 \times Z$) and can be used as a new benchmark for high-resolution volumetric shape completion tasks. Besides the cranium, skull shape completion can also be extended to the facial area.

Acknowledgements. This work was supported by CAMed (COMET K-Project 871132), which is funded by the Austrian Federal Ministry of Transport, Innovation and Technology (BMVIT) and the Austrian Federal Ministry for Digital and Economic Affairs (BMDW) and the Styrian Business Promotion Agency (SFG). Furthermore, the Austrian Science Fund (FWF) KLI 678-B31: "enFaced: Virtual and Augmented Reality Training and Navigation Module for 3D-Printed Facial Defect Reconstructions" and the TU Graz LEAD Project "Mechanics, Modeling and Simulation of Aortic Dissection". Finally, we want to thank the creator of the CQ500 data collection (http://headctstudy.qure.ai/dataset).

References

1. Gall, M., et al.: Cranial Defect Datasets, March 2019. https://figshare.com/articles/Cranial_Defect_Datasets/4659565
2. Egger, J., et al.: Towards the automatization of cranial implant design in cranioplasty. Zenodo (2020). https://doi.org/10.5281/zenodo.3715953
3. Li, J., Pepe, A., Gsaxner, C., Egger, J.: An online platform for automatic skull defect restoration and cranial implant design. arXiv, abs/2006.00980 (2020)
4. Morais, A., Egger, J., Alves, V.: Automated Computer-aided Design of Cranial Implants Using a Deep Volumetric Convolutional Denoising Autoencoder, pp. 151–160, April 2019
5. Dai, A., Qi, C.R., Nießner, M.: Shape completion using 3D-encoder-predictor CNNs and shape synthesis. In: Proceedings of the Computer Vision and Pattern Recognition (CVPR). IEEE (2017)
6. Han, X., Li, Z., Huang, H., Kalogerakis, E., Yu, Y.: High-resolution shape completion using deep neural networks for global structure and local geometry inference. In: IEEE International Conference on Computer Vision (ICCV), October 2017
7. Chang, A.X., et al.: ShapeNet: an information-rich 3D model repository. arXiv preprint arXiv: 1512.03012 (2015)

Automated Virtual Reconstruction of Large Skull Defects using Statistical Shape Models and Generative Adversarial Networks

Pedro Pimentel[1]([✉]), Angelika Szengel[1], Moritz Ehlke[1], Hans Lamecker[1], Stefan Zachow[1,2], Laura Estacio[3], Christian Doenitz[4], and Heiko Ramm[1]

[1] 1000shapes GmbH, Berlin, Germany
{pedro.pimentel,angelika.szengel,moritz.ehlke,
hans.lamecker,stefan.zachow,heiko.ramm}@1000shapes.com
[2] Zuse Institute Berlin (ZIB), Berlin, Germany
[3] San Pablo Catholic University, Arequipa, Peru
laura.estacio@ucsp.edu.pe
[4] Department of Neurosurgery, University Medical Center Regensburg,
Regensburg, Germany
http://www.1000shapes.com

Abstract. We present an automated method for extrapolating missing regions in label data of the skull in an anatomically plausible manner. The ultimate goal is to design patient-specific cranial implants for correcting large, arbitrarily shaped defects of the skull that can, for example, result from trauma of the head.

Our approach utilizes a 3D statistical shape model (SSM) of the skull and a 2D generative adversarial network (GAN) that is trained in an unsupervised fashion from samples of healthy patients alone. By fitting the SSM to given input labels containing the skull defect, a first approximation of the healthy state of the patient is obtained. The GAN is then applied to further correct and smooth the output of the SSM in an anatomically plausible manner. Finally, the defect region is extracted using morphological operations and subtraction between the extrapolated healthy state of the patient and the defective input labels.

The method is trained and evaluated based on data from the MICCAI 2020 AutoImplant challenge. It produces state-of-the art results on regularly shaped cut-outs that were present in the training and testing data of the challenge. Furthermore, due to unsupervised nature of the approach, the method generalizes well to previously unseen defects of varying shapes that were only present in the hidden test dataset.

Keywords: Cranioplasty · Cranial implant design · Skull reconstruction · Statistical shape model (SSM) · Generative adversarial network (GAN) · AutoImplant · Grand Challenge

© Springer Nature Switzerland AG 2020
J. Li and J. Egger (Eds.): AutoImplant 2020, LNCS 12439, pp. 16–27, 2020.
https://doi.org/10.1007/978-3-030-64327-0_3

1   Introduction

This work was created as part of the MICCAI Grand Challenge "AutoImplant"[1]. The goal of this challenge is the comparison of different approaches for designing patient-specific cranial implants to cover large bone defects of the cranial bone. As mentioned by Li et al. [1] in the challenge baseline paper, there is a significant need to move, typically costly and third-party, cranial reconstruction to the Operating Room (OR) - not only from a cost reduction perspective, but also as it might also promote a better fit with the patient, as defects may change over the waiting period due to ossification or osteolysis at the defect edges. Following this, special focus is given to automation and time constraints of the proposed approach in order to facilitate in-OR design and manufacturing, whilst still providing useful results. Fuessinger et al. [2] presented a similar, but only semi-automated, approach to cranial reconstruction using a SSM combined with geometric morphometrics postprocessing, in which manually placed landmarks constrain the possible transformations of the SSM.

Generative adversarial networks (GANs) are a relatively new approach based on adversarial training between two networks [3] known as a generator and a discriminator. The first one is in charge of generating new samples from random noise and the second one tries to discriminate which comes from the real dataset and which one comes from the generator. Kazeminia et al. [4] reviewed current efforts being done in applying GANs in medical imaging, noting their good results in data reconstruction. Although GANs could follow supervised learning, unsupervised learning has also shown promising results in many tasks such as brain lesion segmentation [5] or retina pathology detection [6]. Moreover, GANs produce interesting results for denoising applications [7], which further promotes them as an important resource for post-processing results.

In the work presented here, we adopt an approach for the reconstruction of large bone defects of the pelvic bones used in [8], in which a healthy SSM of the pelvis is employed to predict the healthy shape of the acetabulum after severe pathological change. The user initially provides a mask of the pathological area that is to be ignored during SSM fitting and then by adjusting the SSM to the remaining healthy parts, the model interpolates a likely shape of the bone before the defect. We extend the original SSM approach with an automatic step, thus removing the need for initial user input and automating the entire process. These results are then further improved upon by processing them through a unsupervised GAN trained on skull data.

2   Materials and Methods

2.1   Skull Defect Data

The data provided by the Grand Challenge is split into 100 training and 110 test data sets. Each data set comes as a stack of transversal image slices with

---

[1] https://autoimplant.grand-challenge.org/.

a pixel spacing of approx. 0.5 mm and a slice distance of 0.625 mm. The image data comes in binary format, where foreground voxels represent the skull bone generated from high-resolution CT scans based on a threshold segmentation.

The training set comes separated into three image stacks (see Fig. 1): (1) the full skull without a defect, (2) the skull with an artificially generated defect (defect image), and (3) the isolated defect itself. The defect is fully or partially located on the parietal bone (back of the skull) and has a rectangular shape with straight cuts on the edges. The corners sometimes show round holes.

Fig. 1. Volume rendering of a typical training data set case (id 012). The field of view shows the full skull (grey) and parts of maxilla and mandible. The defect (blue) is provided as a separate label. (Color figure online)

The test set is provided with only the defect images. The first 100 data sets show defects similar to the training data. Whereas the defects of the remaining ten cases vary in position and shape (see Fig. 2).

Fig. 2. Three out of ten additional test cases with varying defects (from left to right: id 103, id 100, id 102).

2.2   Statistical Shape Model of the Human Skull

We generated a statistical shape model (SSM) of the human skull consisting of two surface layers: one surface is representing the outer cortical shell of the skull including the temporal, occipital, frontal, sphenoid, and parietal bones. The second surface represents the dura that is lying directly underneath the inner cortical shell of the skull bones. The SSM surface contains of 27, 500 vertices and 54, 000 triangles.

Our model was generated by automatically fitting an existing SSM of the skull that has the same properties as described above. This model was the result of a previous project that was done in cooperation with the University Medical Center Regensburg. For this earlier work, a skull SSM was generated by a semi-automatic method (described in [9]), where training surfaces are manually decomposed into so called patches, i.e. corresponding anatomical regions with the topology of a disc. This previous SSM contained 18 training data sets only.

In order to avoid the manual effort required for the SSM generation, we established point correspondence over the challenge training data sets by adjusting this previous SSM to the input images (complete skulls). The method used for this fitting is similar to the SSM fit described in the subsequent sections, but only using steps 1 and 2 as there is no defect region that we need to reconstruct.

Performing principal component analysis (PCA) on the resulting surfaces yielded a new SSM represented by its mean (see Fig. 3a) and its principal modes of shape variation (see Fig. 3b). The shape generation and representation is based on the methodology presented in [9]. The SSM trained for this work is purely based on the 100 training data sets provided by the Grand Challenge and no additional data sets were used.

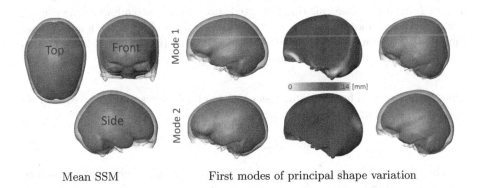

Mean SSM   First modes of principal shape variation

Fig. 3. The SSM of the skull generated from the provided training data.

2.3   GAN for Correcting Local Defects

To remove smaller, localized defects in label volumes of the skull, we introduce an unsupervised approach based on generative adversarial networks (GANs). The proposed networks are trained on individual 2D slices of healthy skull volumes (without defects) such that the generator component of the GAN produces anatomically-plausible 2D labels given defective 2D input.

Architecture. The GAN architecture (Fig. 4) is largely inspired by previous work such as adversarial autoencoders [10], DCGAN [11] and GANomaly [12].

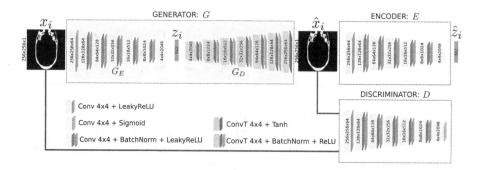

Fig. 4. Proposed GAN architecture with generator G, encoder E, and discriminator D. The generator itself is an autoenconder with encoder component (G_E) and decoder component (G_D).

The generator G is an autoencoder network composed of encoder (G_E) and decoder (G_D) networks. G_E transforms a 2D slice x_i into a lower-dimensional latent space vector z_i of size 512. G_D reconstructs the input x_i from the latent space vector z_i, generating an estimate of the input $\hat{x}_i$. The global encoder component E in turn transforms the generated slice $\hat{x}_i$ back into a lower-dimensional latent space $\hat{z}_i$ while enforcing consistency between z_i and $\hat{z}_i$ in the loss function. Finally, the discriminator component D identifies an input slice of x_i and $\hat{x}_i$ as real or fake respectively for adversarial training.

Loss Functions. The generator loss consists of an adversarial loss, reconstruction loss and latent space consistency loss:

$$\mathcal{L}_G = \mathcal{L}_{adv} + \mathcal{L}_{rec} + \mathcal{L}_{lsc} \tag{1}$$

The adversarial loss L_{adv} is based on feature matching which has shown to reduce the instability of GAN training [13]. It is defined as $\mathcal{L}_{adv} = ||f(D(x_i)) - f(D(G(x_i))||_2$ and measures the similarity between an intermediate layer of $\mathcal{D}$ of input x_i and prediction $\hat{x}_i$. The reconstruction loss L_{rec} is given by the L_1 metric which has demonstrated to produce less blurry results than L_2 [14]. Finally, the latent space consistency loss L_{lsc} aims at minimizing the distance between the two latent spaces z_i and $\hat{z}_i$ [12], and is defined as $\mathcal{L}_{lsc} = ||G_E(x_i) - E(G(x_i))||_2$.

The discriminator loss it is given by the binary cross-entropy loss for a classification problem between the input x_i and prediction $\hat{x}_i$:

$$\mathcal{L}_D = E_{x_i}[\log D(x_i)] + E_{\hat{x}_i}[\log(1 - D(G(x_i)))] \tag{2}$$

Training. The networks were trained simultaneously on $56{,}320$ transverse 2D slices, extracted from the label volumes that showed the full skull without defects in the training data set. 5% of the slices were selected for validation purposes. To match the input resolution of the GAN, the slices were sub-sampled to a resolution of 256×256, and randomly combined into batches of 64 images. The weights were optimized using Adam [15] over 328 epochs (learning rate: 1e−5, β_1: 0.5, β_2: 0.999), at which point the reconstruction loss showed convergence for both the training and validation data.

2.4   Algorithm for Virtual Reconstruction of Skull Defects

Our algorithm can be divided into the following steps depicted in Fig. 5. Each step is described in more detail below.

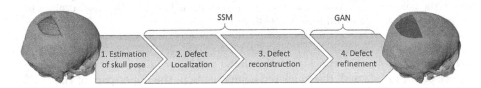

Fig. 5. Overview of the reconstruction pipeline. Steps 2 and 3 are based on adjusting the SSM, whereas step 4 is based on an unsupervised GAN.

Estimation of Skull Pose. As the subsequent SSM-based reconstruction steps require a local initialisation of the shape model within the image data, we perform a pose estimation of the skull. We employ an extension of the generalized Hough transform (GHT) for localisation of 3D shapes as used in [16]. The mean model of the SSM serves as a shape template that is matched with the input image gradients. The pose and scale variation that yields the best match of image gradients and surface normals is considered the initial pose and size of the skull SSM for further matching.

Defect Localisation. The first SSM-adaptation step aims at identifying the defect region, i.e. the parts of the defect skull that are bounding the hole. This is required as the SSM is mainly driven by image features that are sampled along surface normals, resulting in a tendency of the model to get pulled inside the defect area (see Fig. 6a).

To localize the defect, we apply a simple gradient-driven adaptation of the SSM similar to the approach presented in [16]. After finding the parameter set of the SSM (pose, size, shape) that best resembles the instance in the defect image a second deformation step is performed. This second step is used to overcome one limitation of SSMs: new shapes that are not well covered by the SSM training population, cannot be described exactly by the SSM. For this step a graph-cut based regularisation scheme is applied.

After the SSM is fitted to the defect image, the resulting enclosed volume between inner and outer shell is converted to foreground voxels. Subtracting the

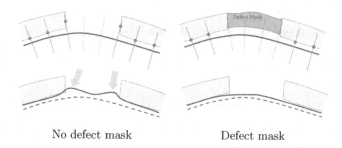

No defect mask   Defect mask

Fig. 6. The SSM will be dragged inside the defect region if image features are detected inside the hole area (a). When the approx. defect area is known by a mask, profiles in its vicinity can be ignored during the fitting (b).

defect image from the reconstructed volume yields an image that contains the defect plus a lot of small disconnected components in the upper part of the skull and larger disconnected components in the base of the skull (see Fig. 7a). To extract the defect from this subtraction image, a morphological opening operation is used to remove small components and artefacts attached to the boundary of the defect. Finally, the initial defect is extracted as a single large component (voxel count >50,000) that has the largest z-coordinate.

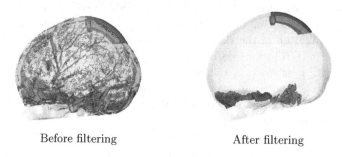

Before filtering   After filtering

Fig. 7. Defect extraction after SSM fitting. Subtracting the defect skull from the segmentation leads to a lot of small and large connected components (a). After performing a morphological opening and component size filtering, only one large component remains at the top of the skull.

Defect Reconstruction. The actual SSM-based defect reconstruction is a repetition of the previous 'defect localisation' step with one change: to prevent the SSM from being pulled inside the defect zone, the initial defect from the previous step is used to generate a mask which defines the defect boundary (see Fig. 6b). Any normal profile that passes through this area will be ignored during the fitting process. The extracted defect fits better to the boundary of the defect and shows an overall smoother extrapolation.

However, as the small area at the vicinity of the defect is ignored small imperfections still remain, especially in the transition area, e.g. small discontinuities between native and reconstructed bone. To this end, the SSM-based defect reconstruction is passed on to an unsupervised GAN for post-processing.

Defect Refinement. The idea behind the refinement step is to further correct and smooth the reconstructed defect region by applying the generator network of the 2D GAN introduced in the previous sections. For this purpose, we first combine (logical OR) the binary labels from the SSM-based defect reconstruction and the input defect skull (without the defect) label volume. 2D slices are then extracted in transversal plane from the merged volumes, converted to floating-valued grey-channel images, and fed slice-by-slice to the generator (see also Fig. 4). The output images are re-combined into label volumes and thresholded to obtain a label prediction of the skull without defect. We found that a threshold in the first quantile of the output distribution of the generator works best for the given application. Finally, the subtraction and opening operations from the previous step are repeated to filter for the defect region and to obtain the virtual reconstruction outcome.

3   Experiments and Results

Experiments on Training Data. For a first internal evaluation of our pipeline, based on the training data we performed a test run and measured the dice score (DSC) and relative volume difference (VD). As the SSM was generated from the training data, all experiments were executed in a leave-one-out fashion, i.e. the respective training data set to be reconstructed got removed from the SSM.

The average scores of DSC and VD of the training set results are given in Table 1. With the ground truth defect (GTD) and the reconstructed defect (RD) as input the VD is defined as $(V_{GTD} - V_{RD})/V_{RD}$. A value of zero stands for equal volume sizes while a negative value indicates over estimation of the defect size and vice versa. DSC is also visualized in a box-plot for every subsequent step of the pipeline (see Fig. 8a).

Color coding the surface distance from ground truth implant to the reconstruction does not reveal any specific region of the defect where deviations typically occur (see Fig. 8b). A visual impression of different reconstruction results is given in Fig. 9.

Table 1. Scores on training data.

	Localisation	Reconstruction	Refinement
mean DSC (stdev)	0.889 (0.039)	0.909 (0.033)	0.913 (0.032)
mean VD	0.078	0.027	−0.02

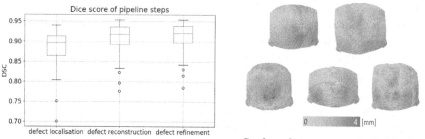

Dice score on training cases   Surface distance on selected train-
                                      ing cases

Fig. 8. (a) Training case results for single pipeline step. (b) Implant ground truth for training cases (from upper left to lower right 000, 020, 025, 041, 099) with color map of measured surface distance to the reconstruction displayed in red. (Color figure online)

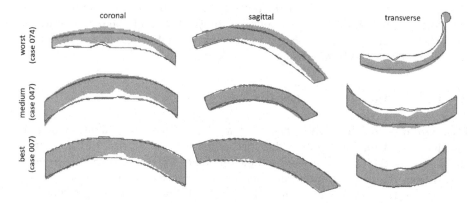

Fig. 9. Different training set reconstructions in terms of DSC (green: ground truth, red line: SSM; blue line: GAN): the worst DSC result also shows a strong mismatch in the middle part of the defect. (Color figure online)

Close to the transition area between native and virtually reconstructed bone, the GAN result shows an improvement in terms of continuity (see Fig. 10).

Experiments on Testing Data. We also tested our pipeline on a second test data set for which no ground truth was given. None of this data was used in any way for training the SSM or GAN. Therefore, a leave-one-out strategy was neither needed nor applied here. The results calculated by the organisers of this challenge are summarized in Table 2 and also the variation of all 110 cases is visualized with box plots in Fig. 11.

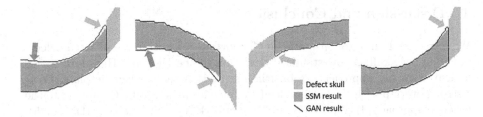

Fig. 10. Examples of results obtained from the SSM and subsequent GAN step: The GAN results show a better transition to the remaining bone close to the defect boundary (green arrows). Further away from the defect boundary stronger deviations between SSM and GAN results can be observed (yellow arrows). (Color figure online)

Table 2. Scores on testing data.

	Test case (100)	Test case (10)	Overall (110)
mean DSC	0.917	0.919	0.917
mean HD	4.336	3.987	4.304

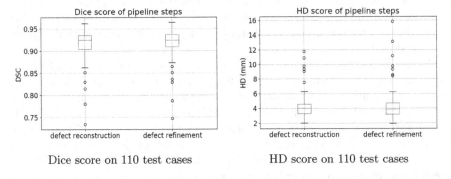

Dice score on 110 test cases   HD score on 110 test cases

Fig. 11. (a) DSC box-plot of all 110 training cases for final SSM fit (defect reconstruction) and GAN (defect refinement). (b) HD (mm) score box-plot of all 110 training cases for final SSM fit (defect reconstruction) and GAN (defect refinement).

Runtime. For the experiments, we used a workstation equipped with a 2.30 GHz Intel Core i5 processor, as well as server hardware with two Intel Xeon CPUs and four NVIDIA Quadro RTX 6000 GPUs. SSM-based reconstruction on the workstation took between 7 to 12 min per case, including both SSM fitting stages. The GAN-based inference step needed two minutes per case, utilizing the GPU hardware on the server.

4   Discussion and Conclusion

We introduced an automatic pipeline for virtual reconstruction of large defects of the upper skull. A low standard deviation in the Dice and Hausdorff scores indicate that our approach is robust in a sense that the resulting implant shows a strong overlap with the original healthy bone for all subjects. Compared to the baseline approach [1] (reported scores on network N_2: DSC: 0.8555, HD: 5.1825), our method shows an improvement (DSC: 0.917, HD: 4.336).

Applying our GAN approach to the SSM-based defect slightly improves the Dice score. This behaviour can be especially observed in the transition from native bone to virtually reconstructed defect (see Fig. 10). As our GAN is only trained on a single slice direction, we expect it to show further improvement if a multi-slice or even 3D approach is used.

On test cases with different characteristic, our method achieves equally good results as on the 'training-like' cases. This makes it a suitable approach to fix large defects of arbitrary shape on the top and back of the skull bone. A visual inspection of the surface distances on the training data revealed that the areas of largest deviations are arbitrary, i.e. there is no typical location where our approach shows the largest error. This is an indicator that the local anatomical variations inside such large defects are only weakly correlated with the surrounding healthy bone. This could pose a natural boundary for any method that heavily relies on statistical shape knowledge.

For the clinical application of such an approach it is important to consider two additional requirements in the future: First, it might be beneficial if the implant is minimally smaller at the edges (e.g. 0.3 mm) to allow for an easy insertion into the defect. Second, due to thick scarring, which can be seen intraoperatively, it may be better to manufacture the implant much thinner (e.g. only 5 mm thick). As our approach allows differentiation between the defect rim, inner cortical and outer cortical shell, adapting the method to fulfill those constraints is straight forward, e.g. by localized morphological operations.

One of the main motivation of this challenge was to propose a method that could potentially be used to create an implant intraoperatively. Our approach can produce a proposal for an implant in a few minutes. Together with the accuracy and reliability of our method, we consider this requirement to be fulfilled.

References

1. Li, J., Pepe, A., Gsaxner, C., von Campe, G., Egger, J.: A baseline approach for AutoImplant. In: The MICCAI 2020 Cranial Implant Design Challenge. arXiv: 2006.12449 (2020)
2. Fuessinger, M.A., et al.: Planning of skull reconstruction based on a statistical shape model combined with geometric morphometrics. Int. J. Comput. Assist. Radiol. Surg. **13**(4), 519–529 (2017). https://doi.org/10.1007/s11548-017-1674-6
3. Goodfellow, I., et al.: Generative adversarial nets. In: Advances in Neural Information Processing Systems, vol. 27, pp. 2672–2680 (2014)

4. Kazeminia, S., et al.: GANs for medical image analysis. arXiv preprint arXiv:1809.06222 (2018)
5. Baur, C., Wiestler, B., Albarqouni, S., Navab, N.: Deep autoencoding models for unsupervised anomaly segmentation in brain MR images. In: Crimi, A., Bakas, S., Kuijf, H., Keyvan, F., Reyes, M., van Walsum, T. (eds.) BrainLes 2018. LNCS, vol. 11383, pp. 161–169. Springer, Cham (2019). https://doi.org/10.1007/978-3-030-11723-8_16
6. Schlegl, T., Seeböck, P., Waldstein, S., Langs, G., Schmidt-Erfurth, U.: f-AnoGAN: fast unsupervised anomaly detection with generative adversarial networks. In: Medical Image Analysis, vol 54, pp. 30–44 (2019)
7. Yi, X., Babyn, P.: Sharpness-aware low-dose CT denoising using conditional generative adversarial network. J. Digit. Imaging **31**, 655–669 (2018)
8. Hettich, G., et al.: Method for quantitative assessment of acetabular bone defects. J. Orthop. Res. **37**, 181–189 (2019)
9. Lamecker, H., Seebaß, M., Hege, H.-C., Deuflhard, P.: A 3D statistical shape model of the pelvic bone for segmentation. In: Proceedings of SPIE Medical Imaging, vol. 5370, pp. 1341–1351 (2004)
10. Makhzani, A., Shlens, J., Jaitly, N., Goodfellow, I., Frey, B.: Adversarial autoencoders. arXiv preprint arXiv:1511.05644 (2015)
11. Radford, A., Metz, L., Chintala, S.: Unsupervised representation learning with deep convolutional generative adversarial networks. arXiv preprint arXiv:1511.06434 (2015)
12. Akcay, S., Atapour-Abarghouei, A., Breckon, T.P.: GANomaly: semi-supervised anomaly detection via adversarial training. In: Jawahar, C.V., Li, H., Mori, G., Schindler, K. (eds.) ACCV 2018. LNCS, vol. 11363, pp. 622–637. Springer, Cham (2019). https://doi.org/10.1007/978-3-030-20893-6_39
13. Salimans, T., Goodfellow, I., Zaremba, W., Cheung, V., Radford, A., Chen, X.: Improved techniques for training GANs. In: Advances in Neural Information Processing Systems, pp. 2234–2242 (2016)
14. Isola, P., Zhu, J.Y., Zhou, T., Efros, A.A.: Image-to-image translation with conditional adversarial networks. In: Proceedings of the IEEE Conference on Computer Vision and Pattern Recognition, pp. 1125–1134 (2017)
15. Diederik, P.K., Lei Ba, J.: Adam: a method for stochastic optimization. arXiv preprint arXiv:1412.6980 (2014)
16. Seim, H., Kainmueller, D., Heller, M., Lamecker, H., Zachow, S, Hege, H.-C.: Automatic segmentation of the pelvic bones from CT data based on a statistical shape model. In: Eurographics Workshop on Visual Computing for Biomedicine, pp. 93–100 (2008)

Cranial Implant Design Through Multiaxial Slice Inpainting Using Deep Learning

Haochen Shi[1] (ID) and Xiaojun Chen[2](✉) (ID)

[1] School of Electronic Information and Electrical Engineering, Shanghai Jiao Tong University,
Shanghai, China
jcsyshc@sjtu.edu.cn
[2] School of Mechanical Engineering, Shanghai Jiao Tong University, Shanghai, China
xiaojunchen@sjtu.edu.cn

Abstract. Cranial implant design can be thought as a 3D shape completion task predicting the missing part of a defective cranium, which is a time-consuming task in traditional methods. This paper proposes a deep convolutional neural network (CNN) based method which predicts the implant from a binary voxel image of a defective skull. Three networks with the same structure are trained for inpainting sagittal, coronal, and horizontal slices of the defective skull, respectively. After skull size regularization and slice extraction, inpainting results from one or more axes are used to synthesize the final binary implant voxel image. Cross-validation shows that the proposed method has a good performance in the cranial implant design task in terms of both Dice similarity coefficient (DSC) and Hausdorff distance (HD).

Keywords: Cranial implant design · Shape completion · Deep learning

1 Introduction

Cranial defects can be caused by trauma or brain tumors. To recover the function of the cranium and considering aesthetic factors, the implant should make the repaired cranium as similar as possible to the original undamaged one. Under these demands, the cranial implant design task can be thought as a 3D shape completion task on incomplete binary cranial voxel images.

Dedicated CAD software and sophisticated procedures are commonly used in manual patient-specific implants design methods [1–4], while statistical shape models (SSMs) [5] and volumetric deep convolutional neural networks (3D-CNN) [6, 7] provide fully or semi-automatic solutions to this problem. However, limited by the memory capacity of the graphics cards, the resolution of 3D-CNN is low, and the network cannot be very deep. Besides, there is also an online platform dedicated for this task [8]. Other 3D shape completion methods are commonly based on point clouds [9, 10], signed distance functions (SDF) [11] and depth images [12], but few of them have been applied to this task.

© Springer Nature Switzerland AG 2020
J. Li and J. Egger (Eds.): AutoImplant 2020, LNCS 12439, pp. 28–36, 2020.
https://doi.org/10.1007/978-3-030-64327-0_4

One commonly used cranial implant design method utilizes the symmetry of the skull, which mirrors the defective cranium across the sagittal symmetric plane and uses Boolean operation to get the implant [1, 4, 14]. However, this method cannot output the complete implant if the defect crosses the symmetry plane and dislocations will sometimes be found around the junction, since human craniums are not fully symmetric.

2 Methodology

The proposed method generates implants by synthesizing slice inpainting results from different axes together with some simple preprocessing and postprocessing. To be specific, the skull region of an input voxel image containing a defective cranium is first enlarged to the same dimension. Then three 2D-CNN with the same structure are used to predict implants from defective slices taken from three different axes, respectively. Next, by synthesizing these inpainting results from one or more axes, an enlarged cranial implant is obtained. Finally, after a shrinking operation which inverses the enlarging operation, the final cranial implant is gained (Fig. 1).

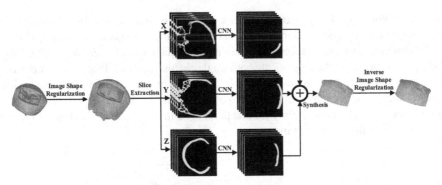

Fig. 1. The overall workflow of the proposed methods.

2.1 Dataset

The dataset was taken from the AutoImplant Challenge [15], which contains one training set with 100 cases and one testing set with 110 cases. Each case in the training set has three binary voxel images of the complete and defective cranium and its corresponding implant, one for each, while only images of defective cranium are provided for cases in the testing set. 200 defective images have the similar type of defects, which are called "normal defects" in this paper and the rest 10 have more complex defects, which are called "abnormal defects".

2.2 Preprocessing

Image Shape Regularization. The binary voxel images in the datasets represent the segmented cranium with 1 and others with 0. And the bounding box of a voxel image is the smallest cuboid region which is parallel to the coordinate axes and encloses all voxels with value 1. The skull region of an image is the bounding box of it plus some margins to ensure that the predicted implant can fall into the skull region completely in case the image contains a defective cranium and necessary. The image shape regularization proposed in this paper means resizing the skull region of different images to the same dimension. In order to make slices from different axes to have the same dimension, the regularized dimension was chosen to be $512 \times 512 \times 512$.

Slice Extraction. This paper denotes the three coordinate axes of the voxel image by X, Y and Z axis. In the proposed method, slice extraction is performed on each voxel image after image shape regularization from X, Y and Z axis respectively and the results are stored into three parts, one for each axis.

2.3   Slice Inpainting

A deep learning network is proposed to predict an implant image from a defective skull slice and data augmentation is used during training to ease overfitting.

Network Structure. The proposed network structure is illustrated in Fig. 2 and Fig. 3 and it is essentially a convolutional neural network (CNN) of the denoising autoencoder (DAE) structure with an additional auxiliary path and the channel attention mechanism. The input and output of the network are both single channel images of the same dimension 512×512 but with different value ranges. The input image is binary skull slice with values 0 and 1, while each pixel in the output image has a value range from 0 to 1 and larger value means higher certainty for that pixel to be in the implant. This type of image is called probability image in this paper.

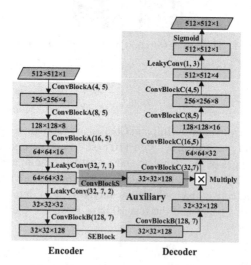

Fig. 2. Overall structure of the proposed network. Red parallelogram denotes input defective image. Green parallelogram denotes output implant image. Texts next to the arrows denote the operation blocks used in the dataflow. (Color figure online)

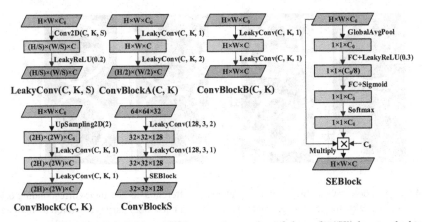

Fig. 3. Operation blocks' definition. "C" denotes the number of channels, "K" denotes the kernel size used in the convolution layers (same value for x and y dimensions), and "S" denotes the strides of convolution operation (same value for x and y dimensions).

Data Augmentation. The proposed data augmentation methods are based on statistical analysis of the shape of all the implant and defective cranium images in the dataset, which is trying to generate fake defective skull slices from complete skull slices. Taking the X axis for example, the proposed statistical analysis is simply calculating the bounding boxes of the implant regions in each implant slice from the X axis together with the varying ranges of some basic geometric properties of these bounding boxes, including their width, height and four boundary positions. In the training phase, a fake defective skull slice is obtained by masking out a randomly generated rectangle region (mask) of a real complete skull slice and the corresponding implant image is obtained by Boolean difference operation on them. Data augmentation schemes in this paper mean different strategies to generate the mask and they vary with different axes and different types of defects. As shown in Fig. 4 and Fig. 5, there are two sets of masks for normal and abnormal defects, respectively. For the normal defects, different data augmentation schemes are used for different axes and these masks are trying to generate defective slices similar to those in the original dataset, thus their sizes and positions are constrained by the aforementioned geometric properties. For the abnormal defects, different axes use the same three schemes, whose masks' sizes and positions vary in a wider range than the normal defects' masks to enhance the inpainting capacity.

Training. The proposed networks are trained on a computer with one GTX 1080 graphics card and one GTX 960 graphics card and the batch size was set to be 8. The loss function is chosen to be dice loss [13] and four optimizer and learning rate pairs are used four training, which are Adam@0.0005, Adam@0.0002, SGD@0.0001 and SGD@0.00005. These pairs are used successively, and parameter weights are saved after every epoch. Starting with Adam@0.0005, when the validation loss start to ascent and three tolerance epochs have passed, parameter weights with the lowest validation loss are reloaded and the next pair is used to repeat the aforementioned process until the last pair is used or the validation loss cannot descent anymore.

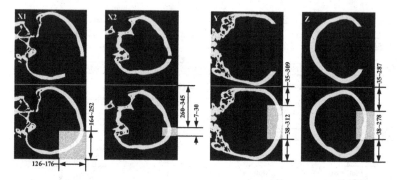

Fig. 4. Typical defective images of normal defects of different axes and their corresponding data augmentation masks. In the mask generation process, if a mask boundary is anchored to an image boundary in the figure, that mask boundary is fixed to that image boundary. If a mask boundary is constrained by a length range, the true position of that mask boundary is determined by randomly choose a length in the length range. If a mask boundary is unconstrained, then its true position is guaranteed to let the mask cut through the skull completely.

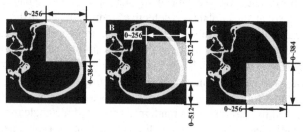

Fig. 5. Data augmentation masks for abnormal defects. Three mask types (A, B and C) are used for all X, Y and Z axis.

2.4 Synthesis

By stacking the predicted implant slices of one axis together in the original order, an implant voxel probability image is obtained, whose value of each voxel ranges from 0 to 1. Then, these voxel images from different axes are combined to form a multi-channel voxel image and the binary version of it is calculated by the following strategy: For each voxel, if the sum of all the channels is greater than half of the channel number, then its final value is 1, otherwise the value is 0. In the other words, let $P^{(1)}$, $P^{(2)}$, $P^{(3)}$ denote the stacked voxel probability image from different axes, the predicted implant voxel image P is determined by the following equations.

- If three axes are used for prediction:

$$P = \begin{cases} 1, & \frac{P^{(1)}+P^{(2)}+P^{(3)}}{3} \geq \frac{1}{2} \\ 0, & \text{others} \end{cases} \qquad (1)$$

- If two axes are used for prediction:

$$P = \begin{cases} 1, & \frac{P^{(1)}+P^{(2)}}{2} \geq \frac{1}{2} \\ 0, & \text{others} \end{cases} \tag{2}$$

- If only one axis is used for prediction:

$$P = \begin{cases} 1, & P^{(1)} \geq \frac{1}{2} \\ 0, & \text{others} \end{cases} \tag{3}$$

Then, after a simple resize transformation which inverses the image shape regularization process mentioned in the preprocessing part, the final implant voxel image is obtained.

3 Results

Cross-validation shows that the synthesized results from the combination of X and Y axis have the lowest mean Hausdorff distance (HD) among all the different combinations, with only slightly lower Dice similarity coefficient (DSC) than the combination of X, Y and Z axis. Besides, the defective slices of Z axis of abnormal defects are too sophisticated and are hard to generate through a simple rectangle mask. Thus, the submitted implant images are all synthesized from X and Y axis, but different versions of network parameter weights are still used in the inpainting of slices from normal and abnormal defects separately. Note that the networks for inpainting normal and abnormal defects have the same network structure and the only difference is in the training phase, where different data augmentation schemes are used for them, respectively. For those defective skull images which have non-straight cutting edges, extra processes must be done for the network to work properly, such as manually enlarging the defective region to make the cutting edge straight and using Boolean operations to erase the overlapping part.

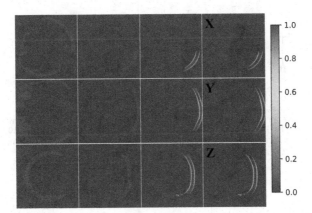

Fig. 6. Plots of 2D slice inpainting results from three axes. From left to right: the input defective skull slices; the ground truth implant slices; the predicted probability implant slices; the absolute-valued difference between the prediction and ground truth.

Figure 6 demonstrates the slice inpainting results of different axes and Fig. 7 demonstrates the visual difference of the synthesized results of different axes combinations. The evaluation results of the 110 testing cases is shown in Table 1 and Fig. 8.

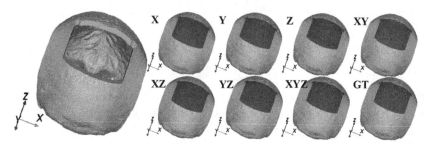

Fig. 7. 3D Plots of synthesized results of different axes' combinations. Streak artifacts caused by slice-wise inpainting can be seen most obviously from single axis' results (X, Y, Z) and the outer surface of three axes' result (XYZ) is smoothest visually.

Table 1. The quantitative results of the 110 testing cases (100 with normal defects and 10 with abnormal defects)

	Test case (100)	Test case (10)	Overall (110)
Mean DSC (%)	93.07	92.38	93.06
Mean HD (mm)	3.66	4.09	3.70

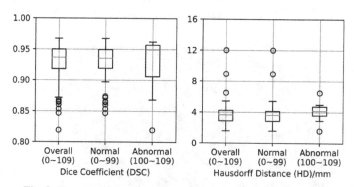

Fig. 8. Boxplot of the quantitative results of the 110 testing cases.

4   Conclusion

This paper proposed a novel cranial implant design method which can predicte the 3D implant from inpainting 2D slices of different axes. The main part of the proposed method, which was responsible for generating the implant, were fully automated, hence it might be useful in reducing the workload of cranial implant designers.

Acknowledgements. This work was supported by the National Key R&D Program of China (No. 2017YFB1302900), National Natural Science Foundation of China (Nos. 81971709, 81828003 and M-0019;82011530141), the Foundation of Science and Technology Commission of Shanghai Municipality (No. 19510712200), and Shanghai Jiao Tong University Foundation on Medical and Technological Joint Science Research (Nos. ZH2018ZDA15, YG2019ZDA06 and ZH2018QNA23).

References

1. Ming-Yih, L., Chong-Ching, C., Chao-Chun, L., Lun-Jou, L., Yu-Ray, C.: Custom implant design for patients with cranial defects. IEEE Eng. Med. Biol. Mag. **21**, 38–44 (2002)
2. Dean, D., Min, K.-J.: Computer aided design of cranial implants using deformable templates (2003)
3. Scharver, C., Evenhouse, R., Johnson, A., Leigh, J.: Pre-surgical cranial implant design using the PARIS/spl trade/prototype. In: IEEE Virtual Reality 2004, pp. 199–291. IEEE (2004)
4. Chen, X., Xu, L., Li, X., Egger, J.: Computer-aided implant design for the restoration of cranial defects. Sci. Rep. **7**, 4199 (2017)
5. Fuessinger, M.A., et al.: Planning of skull reconstruction based on a statistical shape model combined with geometric morphometrics. Int. J. Comput. Assist. Radiol. Surg. **13**(4), 519–529 (2017). https://doi.org/10.1007/s11548-017-1674-6
6. Morais, A., Egger, J., Alves, V.: Automated computer-aided design of cranial implants using a deep volumetric convolutional denoising autoencoder. In: Rocha, Á., Adeli, H., Reis, L.P., Costanzo, S. (eds.) WorldCIST'19 2019. AISC, vol. 932, pp. 151–160. Springer, Cham (2019). https://doi.org/10.1007/978-3-030-16187-3_15
7. Li, J., Pepe, A., Gsaxner, C., Campe, G., Egger, J.: A baseline approach for AutoImplant: the MICCAI 2020 cranial implant design challenge. In: Syeda-Mahmood, T., Drechsler, K., et al. (eds.) CLIP/ML-CDS -2020. LNCS, vol. 12445, pp. 75–84. Springer, Cham (2020). https://doi.org/10.1007/978-3-030-60946-7_8
8. Li, J., Pepe, A., Gsaxner, C., Egger, J.: An online platform for automatic skull defect restoration and cranial implant design (2020)
9. Peng, Y., Chang, M., Wang, Q., Qian, Y., Zhang, Y., Wei, M., Liao, X.: Sparse-to-dense multi-encoder shape completion of unstructured point cloud. IEEE Access **8**, 30969–30978 (2020)
10. Yu, Y., Huang, Z., Li, F., Zhang, H., Le, X.: Point encoder GAN: a deep learning model for 3D point cloud inpainting. Neurocomputing **384**, 192–199 (2020)
11. Park, J.J., Florence, P., Straub, J., Newcombe, R., Lovegrove, S.: DeepSDF: learning continuous signed distance functions for shape representation. In: Proceedings of the IEEE Conference on Computer Vision and Pattern Recognition, pp. 165–174 (2019)
12. Hu, T., Han, Z., Zwicker, M.: 3D shape completion with multi-view consistent inference. arXiv preprint arXiv:1911.12465 (2019)

13. Sudre, Carole H., Li, W., Vercauteren, T., Ourselin, S., Jorge Cardoso, M.: Generalised dice overlap as a deep learning loss function for highly unbalanced segmentations. In: Cardoso, M.J., et al. (eds.) DLMIA/ML-CDS -2017. LNCS, vol. 10553, pp. 240–248. Springer, Cham (2017). https://doi.org/10.1007/978-3-319-67558-9_28
14. Egger, J., et al.: Interactive reconstructions of cranial 3D implants under MeVisLab as an alternative to commercial planning software. PLoS ONE **12**, e0172694 (2017)
15. Egger, J., et al.: Towards the automatization of cranial implant design in cranioplasty. Zenodo (2020)

Cranial Implant Design via Virtual Craniectomy with Shape Priors

Franco Matzkin[1](✉), Virginia Newcombe[2], Ben Glocker[3], and Enzo Ferrante[1]

[1] Research Institute for Signals, Systems and Computational Intelligence,
sinc(i), CONICET, FICH-UNL, Santa Fe, Argentina
`fmatzkin@sinc.unl.edu.ar`
[2] Division of Anaesthesia, Department of Medicine, University of Cambridge,
Cambridge, UK
[3] BioMedIA, Imperial College London, London, UK

Abstract. Cranial implant design is a challenging task, whose accuracy is crucial in the context of cranioplasty procedures. This task is usually performed manually by experts using computer-assisted design software. In this work, we propose and evaluate alternative automatic deep learning models for cranial implant reconstruction from CT images. The models are trained and evaluated using the database released by the AutoImplant challenge, and compared to a baseline implemented by the organizers. We employ a simulated virtual craniectomy to train our models using complete skulls, and compare two different approaches trained with this procedure. The first one is a direct estimation method based on the UNet architecture. The second method incorporates shape priors to increase the robustness when dealing with out-of-distribution implant shapes. Our direct estimation method outperforms the baselines provided by the organizers, while the model with shape priors shows superior performance when dealing with out-of-distribution cases. Overall, our methods show promising results in the difficult task of cranial implant design.

Keywords: Skull reconstruction · Self-supervised learning · Decompressive craniectomy · Shape priors

1 Introduction

Crainoplasty is a surgical procedure aimed at repairing a skull vault defect by insertion of a bone or nonbiological implant (e.g. metal or plastic) [1]. Such skull defect may exist due to different reasons, like a brain tumor removal procedure or a decompressive craniectomy surgery following a traumatic brain injury [12]. Cranial implant design is usually performed by experts using computer-aided design software specifically tailored for this task [2]. The AutoImplant challenge, organized for the first time at MICCAI 2020, aims at bench-marking the latest developments in computational methods for cranial implant reconstruction. In

© Springer Nature Switzerland AG 2020
J. Li and J. Egger (Eds.): AutoImplant 2020, LNCS 12439, pp. 37–46, 2020.
https://doi.org/10.1007/978-3-030-64327-0_5

this work, we propose and evaluate two approaches to solve this task using deep learning models.

Previous works on skull and cranial implant reconstruction suggest that deep learning models are good candidates to solve this task. In [13] a denoising autoencoder was used to perform skull reconstruction, following an approach similar to the recently proposed Post-DAE method [6,7]. In this case, a denoising autoencoder is trained to reconstruct full skulls from corrupted versions. However, the model proposed in [13] works with skulls extracted from magnetic resonance images, can only handle low resolution images and was evaluated on the full-skull reconstruction task. Here we focus on reconstructing the flap only, on skulls extracted from high resolution and anisotropic computed tomography (CT) images. Other approaches rely on a head symmetry assumption and propose to take advantage of it to reconstruct the missing parts by mirroring the complete side of the skull [4]. However, this is not a realistic assumption since missing flaps may occur in both sides simultaneously. Another alternative could be the subtraction of the aligned pre- and post-operative CT scans. Unfortunately, this requires to have access to the pre-operative image, which may not be the case in real clinical scenarios.

Recently, we have proposed [11] a simple virtual craniectomy procedure which enables training different deep learning models in a self-supervised way, given a dataset composed of full skulls. In this work, we compared two different approaches: direct estimation of the implant, or reconstruct-and-subtract (RS) strategies where the full skull is first reconstructed, and then the original image is subtracted from it to generate a difference map. We evaluated different architectures and concluded that direct estimation produces more accurate estimates than RS strategies, since the latter one tends to generate noise in areas far from the flap. A different approach has been introduced by the AutoImplant challenge organizers [9] which also employs deep learning models, but it works in two steps. First, a low resolution version of the image is reconstructed to localize the area where the defected region is located. Then, they extract a 3D patch from the high resolution image and process it using a second neural network trained for fine implant prediction.

In this work, based on the conclusions from [11], we employ a direct estimation method that operates on full skulls which are rigidly registered to an atlas and resampled to an intermediate resolution. Aligning the images allow us to work in a common space which simplifies the reconstruction task. We adapt the virtual craniectomy procedure to account for more realistic flap shapes, similar to the ones introduced in the AutoImplant challenge. Moreover, we propose to incorporate anatomical priors into the standard direct estimation model introduced in [11] by feeding the registered skull atlas as an extra image channel. Previous works [8] have shown that incorporating approximate shape priors as additional image channels is a simple yet effective way to increase the anatomical plausibility of the segmentations, since it provides supplementary context information to the network. We compare the results of our two methods with those obtained by the baseline benchmark model introduced in [9], showing the superiority of our approach.

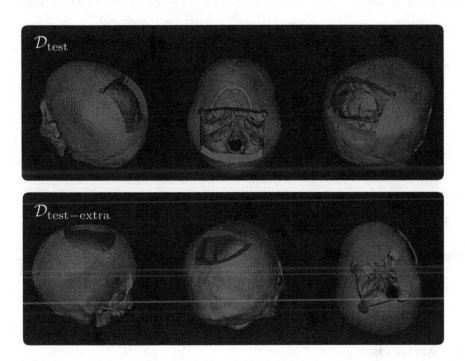

Fig. 1. Examples of images from the $\mathcal{D}_{\text{test}}$ set and $\mathcal{D}_{\text{test}-\text{extra}}$ (out-of-distribution cases). As it can be observed, images from $\mathcal{D}_{\text{test}}$ follow a common pattern, while those in $\mathcal{D}_{\text{test}-\text{extra}}$ present different defects with various shapes.

2 Challenge Description and Database

The AutoImplant challenge organizers provided 100 images for training ($\mathcal{D}_{\text{train}}$) and 110 images for testing. From the 110 test images, 100 of them (denoted here as $\mathcal{D}_{\text{test}}$) have simulated surgical defects which follow the same distribution as the ones on the training images, while the remaining 10 (denoted as $\mathcal{D}_{\text{test}-\text{extra}}$) have defects which do not follow the same distribution (see Fig. 1). The images were selected from the CQ500 public database[1] [3]. They have fixed image dimension in the axial plane (512×512) and a variable number of axial slices Z.

The training dataset ($\mathcal{D}_{\text{train}}$) is composed of triplets ($\mathcal{X}^{\text{full}}, \mathcal{X}^{\text{defected}}, \mathcal{Y}$), where $\mathcal{X}^{\text{full}}$ is the full skull, $\mathcal{X}^{\text{defected}}$ corresponds to the defected skull and $\mathcal{Y}$ to the removed defect that we aim at reconstructing. For the test images, only the $\mathcal{X}^{\text{defected}}$ images were released. We evaluated the proposed methods in

---

[1] The database can be accessed at: http://headctstudy.qure.ai/dataset.

the test images and submitted the results to the organizers, who computed the metrics reported in this paper. It is important to note that, in order to avoid overfitting to the test data, we could submit our results a maximum of 5 times.

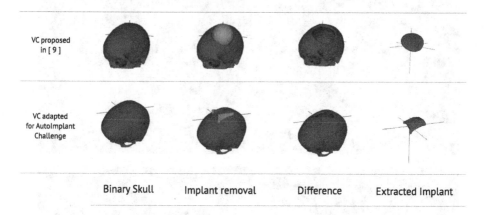

Fig. 2. Modified virtual craniectomy procedure. We incorporated new template shapes for the virtual craniectomy to account for the pattern found in the AutoImplant challenge dataset.

3   Methods

The proposed cranial implant reconstruction methods operate on the space of binary volumetric masks. Such binary skull can be obtained by simply thresholding a brain CT image according to the Hounsfield scale, or applying more sophisticated methods. In the AutoImplant challenge, the skulls were already provided as binary volumes, extracted from the CT images using thresholding and additional post-processing steps (for further details we refer to [9]). Since the training data includes the full skulls, we leveraged the virtual craniectomy procedure proposed in [11] to train our models.

3.1   Virtual Craniectomy and Data Augmentation

Given a full skull, we designed a virtual craniectomy procedure which consists in removing a bone flap using a template located in a random position along its upper part. In [11], spherical template shapes were used. By visual inspection of the AutoImplant training data, we observed that defects tend to follow a pattern given by the intersection of the skull with a cube with two cylinders over the edges perpendicular to the axial planes. So, we designed a variable-size template shape which produces similar defects, as shown in Fig. 2. To increase the diversity of our training procedure, we also included spherical and cubic templates of random sizes (all of the three shapes were selected with equal probability).

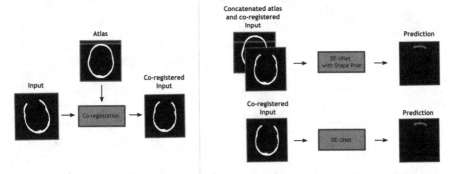

a) Co-registration to a common atlas space | b) Our models: DE-UNet and DE-UNet with Shape Priors

Fig. 3. (a) The images are first registered to an atlas space, and resampled to a common resolution. We store the resulting transform T and its inverse T^{-1}. **(b)** We compare two different approaches for the implant reconstruction task. The first one is a standard DE-UNet model. The second one incorporates a shape prior by considering the atlas as an extra input channel to the network. After prediction, the segmentation mask is mapped-back to the original image space using the inverse transform T^{-1}.

The virtual craniectomy was used as a data augmentation mechanism to generate a variety of training samples from a limited amount of full skulls, resulting in a self-supervised learning approach, where no annotated skull defects are required for training. We also included salt and pepper noise in the input images with probability 0.01. Moreover, we also considered the defective skulls provided by the organizers as part of our datasets (in these cases, virtual craniectomy was not performed). During training, we sampled images coming from both sources: simulated virtual craniectomies and defective skulls provided by the organizers.

3.2 Common Space Alignment

Before training, all the images were rigidly registered to a common space determined by a full skull atlas. It consists in a thresholded version of a full-skull head CT atlas constructed by averaging several healthy head CT images. Such atlas allowed us to normalize the images by resampling them to an intermediate resolution. We chose this resolution to be $0.695 \times 0.695 \times 0.715\,\mathrm{mm}$ (resulting in a volume of $304 \times 304 \times 224$ voxels) because it was the maximum size we managed to fit in GPU memory. Moreover, aligning the images in a common space simplifies the reconstruction task for the neural network, since it can focus on shape variations which are more relevant to the reconstruction task than translations and rotations. We used the FLIRT software package [5] for rigid registration. At test time, given a test defective image $\mathcal{X}_i^{\mathrm{defected}}$, we apply the same registration procedure which returns a transformation T and its inverse T^{-1}. The transformation is applied to the original image $T \circ \mathcal{X}_i^{\mathrm{defected}}$. The estimated skull defect

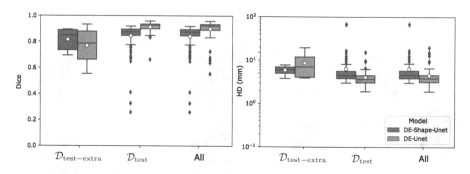

Fig. 4. Comparison of the results for the proposed methods in terms of Dice and Hausdorff Distance (HD). HD is shown in log scale for better visualization.

$\hat{\mathcal{Y}}_i$ is reconstructed in the common space, and the final estimate in the original space is recovered by applying the inverse transformation $\mathcal{T}^{-1} \circ \hat{\mathcal{Y}}_i$.

3.3   Direct Estimation

Our first method is a direct estimation model which follows the same architecture as the DE-UNet used in [11]. It is a standard 3D UNet encoder-decoder architecture with skip connections, trained using a compound loss which combines Dice and cross-entropy terms [14] (for more details, we refer to our work in [11]). After reconstruction, the segmentation is re-mapped to the original resolution using the inverse transform $\mathcal{T}^{-1}$ as previously discussed.

The model is trained using batches with full volume images, pre-aligned in the common space and resampled to an intermediate resolution as previously discussed.

3.4   Direct Estimation with Shape Priors

Since the DE-UNet model is a fully convolutional architecture, the receptive field of the model is mainly determined by the amount of layers and parameters of the pooling and convolution operations. In other words, the local support of the output predictions is restricted to a certain area in the input image. When we have to reconstruct big or out-of-distribution skull defects, it may happen that most of the image support for certain parts of it are background, so the network may have no context to infer the implant shape. To overcome this limitation and make our model robust, we propose to incorporate context via shape priors given as an extra channel to the segmentation network. Previous works [8] have shown that this simple extension can boost the robustness of existing state-of-the-art pixel-wise approaches in medical image segmentation tasks.

We take advantage of the fact that images are co-registered to a common space, and use the same skull atlas as shape prior. After registration, we concatenate the resampled image with the atlas as a extra input channel, and train

Table 1. Quantitative results obtained for the two proposed methods (DE-UNet and DE-Shape-UNet) compared with the two baselines reported by the challenge organizers in [9]. We report the mean Dice and HD values, and the standard deviation in parentheses.

Method	$\mathcal{D}_{test}$ (100)		$\mathcal{D}_{test-extra}$ (10)		Overall	
	Dice	HD (mm)	Dice	HD (mm)	Dice	HD (mm)
Baseline N1 [9]	0.809	5.440	–	–	–	–
Baseline N2 [9]	0.855	5.182	–	–	–	–
DE-UNet	**0.913 (0.038)**	**4.067 (1.762)**	0.769 (0.126)	8.585 (5.128)	**0.900 (0.067)**	**4.477 (2.626)**
DE-Shape-UNet	0.845 (0.107)	6.414 (9.060)	**0.816 (0.078)**	**5.952 (1.258)**	0.842 (0.105)	6.372 (8.648)

the network following the same strategy discussed before. In this case, the shape prior acts as a kind of initialization for the network's output, providing additional context that will be useful specially to reconstruct out-of-distribution defects. We refer to this model as DE-Shape-UNet. Common space alignment and both approaches are depicted in Fig. 3.

3.5 Implementation Details

The models were implemented in Pyhton, using the PyTorch 1.4 library. We trained and evaluated the CNNs using an NVIDIA TITAN Xp GPU with 12 GB of RAM. The same virtual craniectomy and data augmentation procedure was used to train both models. In both cases we used a compound loss function which combines Dice loss and Binary Cross Entropy (BCE) as $L = L_{Dice} + \lambda L_{BCE}$ (parameter λ was set to $\lambda = 1$ by grid search). Both models followed the DE-UNet architecture described in [11]; the only difference between them was that we concatenated the atlas as an extra input channel in the DE-Shape-UNet model. For optimization, we used Adam with initial learning rate of 1e-4. The batch-size was set to 1 for memory restrictions. The models were trained for 50 epochs. The 100 training images were split in 95 images for training and 5 for validation. After 50 epochs, we kept the model that achieved best accuracy in the validation fold.

4   Results

Figure 4 and Table 1 include a quantitative comparison of the results. We report Dice coefficient and Hausdorff distance measured in the $\mathcal{D}_{test}$ (100 images), $\mathcal{D}_{test-extra}$ (10 images) and the whole test dataset. We observe that DE-Shape-UNet presents better performance for out-of-distribution cases ($\mathcal{D}_{test-extra}$), while DE-UNet outperforms the other model in the $\mathcal{D}_{test}$ set. Since the whole test dataset is composed of 100 images from $\mathcal{D}_{test}$ and only 10 images from $\mathcal{D}_{test-extra}$, the DE-UNet model shows better performance in the overall comparison. Moreover, DE-UNet model outperforms the two baseline models (N1 and N2) reported by the organizers in [9]. Figure 5 provides some visual examples for reconstructions obtained with both methods in samples from $\mathcal{D}_{test}$ and $\mathcal{D}_{test-extra}$.

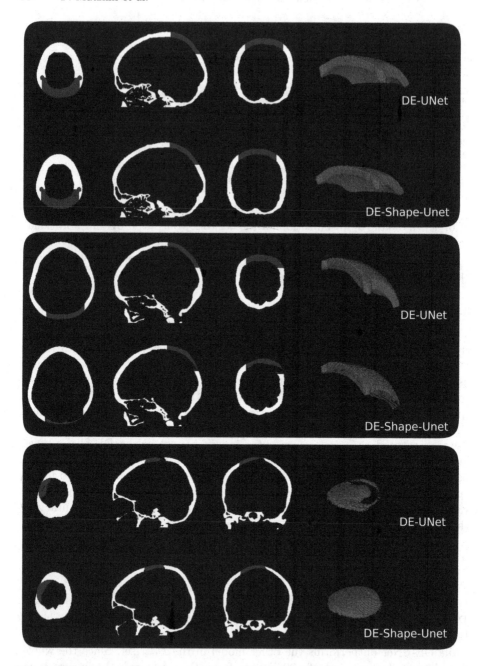

Fig. 5. Examples of different reconstructions from $\mathcal{D}_{\text{test}}$ (cases which follow the same pattern than the training dataset, shown in rows 1 and 2) and $\mathcal{D}_{\text{test}-\text{extra}}$ (out-of-distribution case, shown in row 3). As we can observe, both methods performed well in the image depicted in row 1. For the case in the 2nd row, even if the DE-Shape-UNet model managed to reconstruct the implant, the quality of the reconstruction is lower than that of the DE-UNet. The opposite happened with the image in row 3 (an out-of-distribution case from $\mathcal{D}_{\text{test}-\text{extra}}$) where the model which incorporated shape priors managed to reconstruct the implant, while the DE-UNet failed in this task.

5 Conclusions

In this work, we evaluated two different approaches for cranial implant recon-struction based on deep learning: a direct estimation method and an alterna-tive strategy which incorporates shape priors. We adapted the virtual craniec-tomy procedure proposed in [11] to the defect distribution of the AutoImplant challenge. We found that the simple DE-UNet method produces more accu-rate results for the skull defects which follow the same distribution as those in the training dataset. However, for out-of-distribution cases where the DE-UNet model tends to fail, the use of shape priors increases the robustness of the model, providing additional context to the network. In our implementation, this gain in robustness for out-of-distribution cases was achieved to the detriment of the over-all accuracy. In future work, we plan to study alternative ways to introduce shape priors, e.g. considering deformable registration with anatomical constraints [10] to the atlas space instead of rigid transformations, or incorporating shape priors in a co-registration and segmentation process [15].

Acknowledgments. The authors gratefully acknowledge NVIDIA Corporation with the donation of the Titan Xp GPU used for this research, and the support of UNL (CAID-PIC-50220140100084LI) and ANPCyT (PICT 2018-03907).

References

1. Andrabi, S.M., Sarmast, A.H., Kirmani, A.R., Bhat, A.R.: Cranioplasty: indica-tions, procedures, and outcome-an institutional experience. Surg. Neurol. Int. **8**, 91 (2017)
2. Chen, X., Xu, L., Li, X., Egger, J.: Computer-aided implant design for the restora-tion of cranial defects. Sci. Rep. **7**(1), 1–10 (2017)
3. Chilamkurthy, S., et al.: Development and validation of deep learning algorithms for detection of critical findings in head CT scans. arXiv preprint arXiv:1803.05854 (2018)
4. Hieu, L., et al.: Design for medical rapid prototyping of cranioplasty implants. Rapid Prototyp. J. **9**(3), 175–186 (2003). https://doi.org/10.1108/13552540310477481
5. Jenkinson, M., Bannister, P., Brady, M., Smith, S.: Improved optimization for the robust and accurate linear registration and motion correction of brain images. Neuroimage **17**(2), 825–841 (2002)
6. Larrazabal, A.J., Martínez, C., Glocker, B., Ferrante, E.: Post-DAE: anatomically plausible segmentation via post-processing with denoising autoencoders. IEEE Trans. Medi. Imaging (2020). https://doi.org/10.1109/TMI.2020.3005297
7. Larrazabal, A.J., Martinez, C., Ferrante, E.: Anatomical priors for image segmen-tation via post-processing with denoising autoencoders. In: Shen, D., et al. (eds.) MICCAI 2019. LNCS, vol. 11769, pp. 585–593. Springer, Cham (2019). https://doi.org/10.1007/978-3-030-32226-7_65
8. Lee, M.C.H., Petersen, K., Pawlowski, N., Glocker, B., Schaap, M.: Tetris: template transformer networks for image segmentation with shape priors. IEEE Trans. Med. Imaging **38**(11), 2596–2606 (2019)

9. Li, J., Pepe, A., Gsaxner, C., von Campe, G., Egger, J.: A baseline approach for autoimplant: the miccai 2020 cranial implant design challenge. arXiv preprint arXiv:2006.12449 (2020)

10. Mansilla, L., Milone, D.H., Ferrante, E.: Learning deformable registration of medical images with anatomical constraints. Neural Netw. **124**, 269–279 (2020)

11. Matzkin, F., et al.: Self-supervised skull reconstruction in brain CT images with decompressive craniectomy. In: Martel, A.L., et al. (eds.) MICCAI 2020. LNCS, vol. 12262, pp. 390–399. Springer, Cham (2020). https://doi.org/10.1007/978-3-030-59713-9_38

12. Monteiro, M., et al.: Multiclass semantic segmentation and quantification of traumatic brain injury lesions on head CT using deep learning: an algorithm development and multicentre validation study. Lancet Digit. Health **2**(6), e314–e322 (2020). https://doi.org/10.1016/s2589-7500(20)30085-6

13. Morais, A., Egger, J., Alves, V.: Automated computer-aided design of cranial implants using a deep volumetric convolutional denoising autoencoder. In: Rocha, Á., Adeli, H., Reis, L.P., Costanzo, S. (eds.) WorldCIST'19 2019. AISC, vol. 932, pp. 151–160. Springer, Cham (2019). https://doi.org/10.1007/978-3-030-16187-3_15

14. Patravali, J., Jain, S., Chilamkurthy, S.: 2D-3D fully convolutional neural networks for cardiac MR segmentation. In: Pop, M., et al. (eds.) STACOM 2017. LNCS, vol. 10663, pp. 130–139. Springer, Cham (2018). https://doi.org/10.1007/978-3-319-75541-0_14

15. Shakeri, M., et al.: Prior-based coregistration and cosegmentation. In: Ourselin, S., Joskowicz, L., Sabuncu, M.R., Unal, G., Wells, W. (eds.) MICCAI 2016. LNCS, vol. 9901, pp. 529–537. Springer, Cham (2016). https://doi.org/10.1007/978-3-319-46723-8_61

Deep Learning Using Augmentation via Registration: 1st Place Solution to the AutoImplant 2020 Challenge

David G. Ellis$^{(\boxtimes)}$ ⓘ and Michele R. Aizenberg ⓘ

Department of Neurosurgery, University of Nebraska Medical Center,
Omaha, NE, USA
david.ellis@unmc.edu

Abstract. Automatic cranial implant design can save clinicians time and resources by computing the implant shape and size from a single image of a defective skull. We aimed to improve upon previously proposed deep learning methods by augmenting the training data set using transformations that warped the images into different shapes and orientations. The transformations were computed by non-linearly registering the complete skull images between the 100 subjects in the training data set. The transformations were then applied to warp each of the defective and complete skull images so that the shape and orientation resembled that of a different subject in the training set. One hundred ninety-seven of the registrations failed, resulting in an augmented training set of 9,803 defective and complete skull image pairs. The augmented training set was used to train an ensemble of four U-Net models to predict the complete skull shape from the defective skulls using cross-validation. The ensemble of models performed very well and predicted the implant shapes with a mean dice similarity coefficient of 0.942 and a mean Hausdorff distance of 3.598 mm for all 110 test cases. Our solution ranked first among all participants of the AutoImplant 2020 challenge. The code for this project is available at https://github.com/ellisdg/3DUnetCNN.

Keywords: Deep learning · Shape completion · Augmentation

1 Introduction

Automatic cranial implant design can save clinicians time and resources by computing the implant shape and size needed by a specific patient based on computed tomography imaging of their head [5,6,8,11]. The AutoImplant 2020 Cranial Implant Design Challenge seeks to test varying methods for designing an implant based on an image of a skull with a defect such that part of the skull is missing [7]. The challenge organizers submitted a baseline solution for this challenge in which they experimented with two deep learning solutions [10]. The first solution was to use a cascade style set of models where one model predicts the implant's shape at low-resolution, and another model subsequently refines

© Springer Nature Switzerland AG 2020
J. Li and J. Egger (Eds.): AutoImplant 2020, LNCS 12439, pp. 47–55, 2020.
https://doi.org/10.1007/978-3-030-64327-0_6

that shape at high-resolution. This cascade style solution has the advantage of limiting memory use by only computing the high-resolution implant shape on a cropped image rather than the whole image of the skull. However, the authors noted that overfitting to the training set caused the model to have two key limitations in its ability to generalize to cases outside of the training set [10]. The first limitation was that the model tended to predict the same implant shape for a given skull, even when the location of the defect had been changed. The second limitation was that the model was not able to accurately predict implants for defects that were in different locations and differently shaped than the defects in the training set images. The authors also experimented with using a deep learning network trained to predict the shape of the skull without defects and gave illustrations of how the model appeared to generalize well to cases outside the training set [10].

Inspired by these results, we aimed to implement a deep learning solution that would perform skull completion while learning from a heavily augmented training set. Augmentation is a common approach to expand the size of a training set of data so that a model training on the data will avoid overfitting and will generalize well to cases outside of the training set. Research by Zhao et al. has previously shown that registrations, along with other transformations, can be highly effective at augmenting small training sets of medical images [13]. Zhao et al. showed that the models trained on these augmented training sets performed much better than the models trained without such augmentations [13]. Therefore, we hypothesized that training models on a data set augmented using registrations would produce models that are highly accurate at predicting implant shapes from defective skull images.

2   Methods

2.1   Data

All data was provided by the organizers of the 2020 AutoImplant challenge. A training set was provided with images for 100 subjects along with a test set with images for 110 subjects. The training set consisted of binary images of the complete skull, the defective skull, and the implant for each subject. Renderings of these images are shown in Fig. 1 for an illustrative subject. The testing set consisted of only the defective skulls. One hundred of the testing set subjects had defects similar in location and shape to the training set, while 10 of the testing set subjects had defects with shapes and locations that varied from the defects of the training set.

2.2   Augmentation

Registration. To augment the training set of images, automatic registrations were computed between the skull images for each pair of subjects. This augmentation increases the size of the training set and allows for similarly shaped

Skull   Defective Skull   Implant

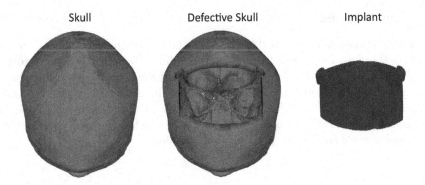

Fig. 1. Three-dimensional mesh renderings of the skull, defective skull, and implant images for a single subject from the training set.

skulls to have varying defect locations. With a training set of 100 images, each individual image can be registered with and warped into the space of 99 other images. Therefore, we attempted to warp the images via registrations and create 9,900 additional training images. Combined with the original training images, this would make an augmented training set of 10,000 images.

The "antsRegistrationSyNQuick.sh" script from the Advanced Normalization Tools (ANTs) package was utilized to compute the combined rigid, affine, and non-linear symmetric image normalization (SyN) warping transformations between skull images [2,3]. For each pair of subjects, the skull of the first subject would be used as the moving image, and the skull of the second subject would be used as the fixed image. The script then computed the transformations to warp the moving image into the fixed image space. The transformations were then applied to the complete and defective skull images to warp the moving images into the fixed image space, and the inverse transforms were used to warp the fixed images into the moving image space. This was repeated for every pair of subjects in the training data set.

Permutation. In order to enhance the model's ability to predict complete skulls for various defect locations, the images were mirrored along the anteroposterior and horizontal directions with a 50% probability for each training iteration.

Scaling. In order to make the model robust to variations in image scaling, the training images were randomly zoomed in and out with a 75% probability for each training iteration.

Translation. In order to make the model robust to variations in the position of the skull within the image, the training images were randomly translated with a 75% probability for each training iteration.

2.3 Preprocessing

All of the images were cropped to remove extra background padding in the images so that only one voxel of background padding around the non-background area remained [1]. In order that all of the data had the same orientation prior to being input into the model, the orientation of the images was set to Right, Anterior, Superior (RAS) [1,4]. After augmentation, the images were resampled down to a size of $176 \times 224 \times 144$ voxels. Apart from the registrations, all preprocessing and augmentation steps were performed at run time.

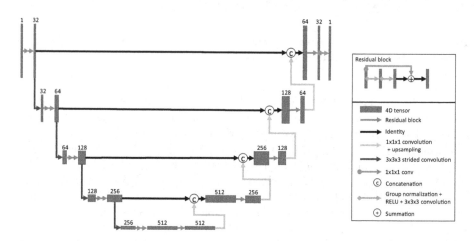

Fig. 2. U-Net model architecture. The number of channels at each step is shown in black.

2.4 Model

We used a U-Net-style convolutional neural network model with residual connections, as shown in Figure 2 [9,12]. Inspired by the research of Myronenko showing that a large receptive field and shallow decoder performed well in the automatic segmentation for brain tumors [12], our model used a large receptive field of $176 \times 224 \times 144$ voxels. Comparatively, the baseline approach used a receptive field of $128 \times 128 \times 64$ voxels [10]. The encoder to the model consisted of five layers, two ResNet style blocks per layer, a base width of 32 channels, dropout, and group normalization. The outputs of each encoding layer were downsampled using a strided convolution before being input into the next layer. The number of channels was doubled at each consecutive layer. Each decoding layer consisted of a single ResNet style block and took as input the output of the previous decoding layer concatenated with the output of the encoding layer at the same resolution. A $1 \times 1 \times 1$ convolution and sigmoid activation were applied to the output of the final decoding layer.

2.5   Training

An ensemble of four models was trained to predict the complete skulls from the defective skulls of the augmented training set using four-fold cross-validation. Each model was trained using two NVIDIA V100 GPUs with 32 gigabytes of memory each. Due to limits on computing resources, training was stopped after seven days.

2.6   Testing

All four models were used to predict the complete skull for all 110 defective skulls from the test set, and the results were averaged across all four models. In order to derive the implant shape from the predicted skull shape, the defective skull was subtracted from the predicted skull. The difference image was then thresholded at 0.5. In order to remove spurious voxels from the predicted implant image, one iteration of morphological opening was performed, and all voxels not connected to the largest connected component were automatically removed.

3   Results

One hundred ninety-seven of the registrations failed, resulting in an augmented training set of 9803 sets of complete and defective skull images. Figure 3 shows an example of augmentations via registrations between two illustrative subjects.

The evaluation of the Dice similarity coefficients (DSC) and Hausdorff distances (HD) was computed by the organizers and reported in Table 1 and Fig. 4. The results are shown for the 100 test cases with defects resembling that of the training cases as well as the 10 test cases with defect shapes and locations that varied from the training set. Qualitatively, the predicted implants matched the shape of the holes in the defective skulls well regardless of defect shape and location, as shown in Fig. 5.

Table 1. Mean Dice similarity coefficient (DSC) and Hausdorff distances (HD) for the 100 test cases with defects resembling the training set as well as for the 10 test cases with defects that varied from the training set in shape and location.

		Test 100	Test 10	Overall
Baseline [10]	DSC	0.856	–	–
	HD (mm)	5.183	–	–
Ours	DSC	**0.944**	0.932	0.942
	HD (mm)	**3.564**	3.934	3.598

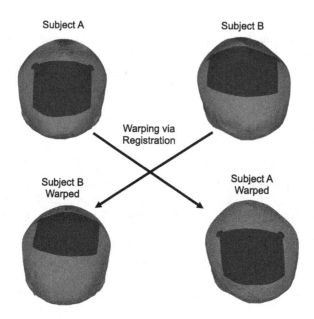

Fig. 3. Example of augmentations produced via registration. The non-linear registration is computed between the skull images of Subject A and Subject B. Then, the defective skull, shown in gray, as well as the implant, shown in red, are warped and translated using the computed non-linear registration. This produces two additional sets of defective skull and implant pairs from every pair of subjects in the training set. (Color figure online)

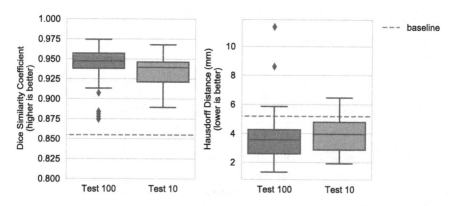

Fig. 4. Distribution of the Dice similarity coefficient and the Hausdorff distances for the 100 test cases and the 10 test cases with defects that varied from the training set in shape and location. For comparison, the average scores for the baseline method on the 100 test cases are shown as the dashed gray line [10].

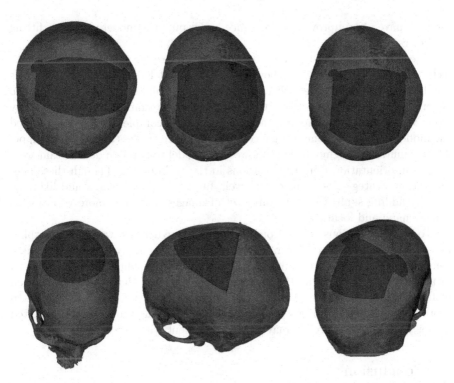

Fig. 5. Examples of defective skulls (gray) and the predicted implants (red) from cases in the 100-case test set (top row) and the 10-case test set (bottom row). The predicted implants fill the defects in the skulls well regardless of defect shape and location. (Color figure online)

4 Discussion

The evaluation metrics for our approach were much better than those reported using the baseline approach without augmentation [10]. For reference, the mean DSC and HD for the baseline approach on the 100 test cases was 0.855 and 5.44 mm [10], respectively, while our approach resulted in DSC and HD measures of 0.944 and 3.564 mm, respectively. This improvement in evaluation metrics likely resulted from a number of improvements we made over the baseline approach. The most prominent improvement was the automatic augmentation of the training data via registration. This augmentation prevents overfitting by allowing similarly shaped skulls to have varying defect locations. By using registrations, we were able to increase the size of the training set from 100 image pairs to 9803 image pairs. While manually creating a training set of this size would require an incredible amount of time, using registrations allows for the augmentations to be computed automatically without manual intervention. Furthermore, the permuting, scaling, and translating augmentations performed during training may have also improved performance by keeping the models from overfitting to the training set.

The DSC and HD scores were only slightly worse for the test set of 10 subjects with unique defects, as shown in Table 1 and Fig. 4, despite the models not being trained on cases with similar defects. The ability of the models to generalize to these cases is likely the result of using a shape completion strategy along with permutation augmentations. The shape completion approach forced the model to focus on generating a complete skull, regardless of the defect shape. The permutation augmentations allowed the model to train on defects that were flipped in orientation from the locations in the training set. Though these augmentation strategies performed very well, further improvement would likely be seen by adding skulls to the training set of images that have more variation in defect shape and location.

To remove spurious voxels from the implant predictions, we used a morphological opening procedure that removed voxels that were only partially or weakly connected to the predicted implant. This was effective but likely also resulted in a loss of edge voxels at the corners of the implant that should have been included in the prediction. Future work could focus on finding a more optimal way to remove these spurious predictions while retaining the correctly predicted corner voxels. One approach may be to experiment with threshold levels.

5   Conclusion

We demonstrated that registrations between anatomical CT images could effectively augment a training set of images for skull shape completion. The model trained on the augmented data set was able to accurately predict complete skull shapes much better than the baseline approach that was trained without using such augmentations.

Acknowledgments. This work was completed utilizing the Holland Computing Center of the University of Nebraska, which receives support from the Nebraska Research Initiative.

References

1. Abraham, A., et al.: Machine learning for neuroimaging with scikit-learn. Front. Neuroinform. **8**, 14 (2014). https://doi.org/10.3389/fninf.2014.00014. https://www.frontiersin.org/article/10.3389/fninf.2014.00014
2. Avants, B.B., Epstein, C.L., Grossman, M., Gee, J.C.: Symmetric diffeomorphic image registration with cross-correlation: evaluating automated labeling of elderly and neurodegenerative brain. Med. Image Anal. **12**(1), 26–41 (2008)
3. Avants, B.B., Tustison, N., Song, G.: Advanced normalization tools (ANTS). Insight J. **2**(365), 1–35 (2009)
4. Brett, M., et al.: freec84: nipy/nibabel: 3.1.1 (2020). https://doi.org/10.5281/zenodo.3924343

5. Chen, X., Xu, L., Li, X., Egger, J.: Computer-aided implant design for the restoration of cranial defects. Sci. Rep. **7**(1), 1–10 (2017)

6. Egger, J., et al.: Interactive reconstructions of cranial 3D implants under MeVisLab as an alternative to commercial planning software. PLoS ONE **12**(3), e0172694 (2017)

7. Egger, J., et al.: Towards the automatization of cranial implant design in cranioplasty (2020). https://doi.org/10.5281/zenodo.3715953

8. Fuessinger, M.A., et al.: Planning of skull reconstruction based on a statistical shape model combined with geometric morphometrics. Int. J. Comput. Assist. Radiol. Surg. **13**(4), 519–529 (2017). https://doi.org/10.1007/s11548-017-1674-6

9. He, K., Zhang, X., Ren, S., Sun, J.: Deep residual learning for image recognition. In: Proceedings of the IEEE Conference on Computer Vision and Pattern Recognition, pp. 770–778 (2016)

10. Li, J., Pepe, A., Gsaxner, C., von Campe, G., Egger, J.: A baseline approach for autoimplant: the miccai 2020 cranial implant design challenge. arXiv preprint arXiv:2006.12449 (2020)

11. Morais, A., Egger, J., Alves, V.: Automated computer-aided design of cranial implants using a deep volumetric convolutional denoising autoencoder. In: Rocha, Á., Adeli, H., Reis, L.P., Costanzo, S. (eds.) WorldCIST'19 2019. AISC, vol. 932, pp. 151–160. Springer, Cham (2019). https://doi.org/10.1007/978-3-030-16187-3_15

12. Myronenko, A.: 3D MRI brain tumor segmentation using autoencoder regularization. In: Crimi, A., Bakas, S., Kuijf, H., Keyvan, F., Reyes, M., van Walsum, T. (eds.) BrainLes 2018. LNCS, vol. 11384, pp. 311–320. Springer, Cham (2019). https://doi.org/10.1007/978-3-030-11726-9_28

13. Zhao, A., Balakrishnan, G., Durand, F., Guttag, J.V., Dalca, A.V.: Data augmentation using learned transformations for one-shot medical image segmentation. In: Proceedings of the IEEE Conference on Computer Vision and Pattern Recognition, pp. 8543–8553 (2019)

Cranial Defect Reconstruction Using Cascaded CNN with Alignment

Oldřich Kodym$^{(\boxtimes)}$ ⓘ, Michal Španěl, and Adam Herout

Department of Computer Graphics and Multimedia, Brno University of Technology,
Božetěchova 2, 612 66 Brno, Czech Republic
ikodym@fit.vutbr.cz

Abstract. Designing a patient-specific cranial implant usually requires reconstructing the defective part of the skull using computer-aided design software, which is a tedious and time-demanding task. This lead to some recent advances in the field of automatic skull reconstruction with use of methods based on shape analysis or deep learning. The AutoImplant Challenge aims at providing a public platform for benchmarking skull reconstruction methods. The BUT submission to this challenge is based on skull alignment using landmark detection followed by a cascade of low-resolution and high-resolution reconstruction convolutional neural network. We demonstrate that the proposed method successfully reconstructs every skull in the standard test dataset and outperforms the baseline method in both overlap and distance metrics, achieving 0.920 DSC and 4.137 mm HD.

Keywords: Skull reconstruction · Shape completion · Cascaded convolutional networks

1 Introduction

Craniectomy is a procedure during which a specific part of the skull is resected and eventually replaced with a cranial implant. When designing the implant, the correct skull shape reconstruction is critical for satisfactory patient outcome. The shape of the implant should make it possible to restore the protective and aesthetic function of the skull and also fit very precisely along the border [7,8]. A successfully reconstructed skull should be mostly indistinguishable from a healthy skull. The original skull shape before the resection is therefore often used as the golden standard of the target reconstructed shape [9].

In case of unilateral defects, techniques based on mirroring the healthy part of the skull to the defect area are often used in combination with a Computer-Aided Design software (CAD) [2]. However, the assumption of perfectly symmetric skull does not hold in most cases and manual corrections are often required. To address these issues, recent methods aim to be completely or mostly automatic and to be able to reconstruct an arbitrary part of the skull, including

© Springer Nature Switzerland AG 2020
J. Li and J. Egger (Eds.): AutoImplant 2020, LNCS 12439, pp. 56–64, 2020.
https://doi.org/10.1007/978-3-030-64327-0_7

bilateral defects. One group of such methods is based on statistical shape models. In combination with geometric morphometrics, both unilateral and bilateral defects can be reconstructed with high precision [4,5]. Another group of methods that has been gaining considerable momentum in recent months is based on deep learning approaches. These methods usually make use of some form of volumetric convolutional neural networks (CNN) with an auto-encoder architecture, although output resolution may often be limited [10–12].

This paper presents a BUT submission to the MICCAI 2020 AutoImplant Challenge [9]. The proposed method is an adaptation of the cascaded reconstruction CNN architecture that has been recently applied to the SkullBreak dataset [6]. Furthermore, the method is extended by an automatic landmark-based registration and a detail-preserving morphological post-processing step. In our experiments, we show how different components of the method affect the reconstruction accuracy on a validation dataset of defective skulls. Finally, we report the results on the full testing dataset of the AutoImplant Challenge.

2   Proposed Method

The proposed method consists of several steps as illustrated in Fig. 1. The landmark detection step and the skull reconstruction step are handled by a 3D CNN model.

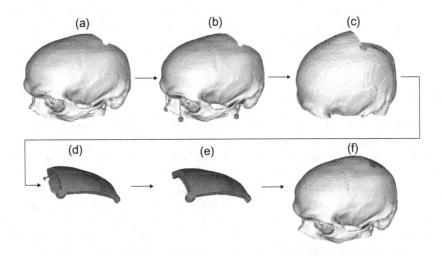

Fig. 1. Overview of the proposed method. In the input skull volume (a) 4 landmarks are detected (b). The skull is transformed (c) so that the detected landmarks (red) are registered to the reference landmarks (green). Then, the skull is reconstructed by estimating the missing shape (d). Finally, the result is post-processed (e) and transformed back into the original skull coordinates (f). (Color figure online)

2.1   Skull Alignment

The defects in the AutoImplant dataset are generated on a static position inside the data volumes and the variability in their shapes and positions comes from the variability of positions of the skulls. When reconstructing the shapes with a volumetric CNN model, this introduces some difficulties. The reconstruction model needs to implicitly learn rotational and translational invariance and it also makes it cumbersome to exploit the symmetric properties of the skulls. To address this, we use scale and rigid transformations to normalize the scale and the position of the skulls.

Unlike the parameters of the scale transform that are known from the CT acquisition process, the parameters of the rigid transformation need to be inferred from the data. We use the positions of four anatomical landmarks, namely the left and right auditory meatus and left and right supraorbital notch (see Fig. 1b), to compute the transform. This allows us to avoid possible complications of using conventional registration methods, such as issues with substantial differences in initial positions of the data volumes and different anatomical regions present in the data.

We trained a simple 3D CNN model for landmark detection with a U-net architecture using the heatmap regression approach [13]. The detection model is illustrated in Fig. 2(left) and its training is further described in Sect. 3. After detecting the landmarks, we find the rigid transform that moves these landmarks onto reference landmarks placed on the xy plane using singular value decomposition [1]. Even if one landmark is not detected either because of the detection model failure or because of a skull defect, such missing detection can usually be identified [3] and the missing landmark position can be computed from the other three landmarks.

2.2   Skull Reconstruction

The skull reconstruction model takes the aligned binary defective skull data as an input and produces the missing part of the skull as an output. The model consists of two 3D CNNs with modified U-net architecture that are trained using the soft Dice loss. Both networks have additional max-pooling and up-sampling steps as compared to U-net to increase the field of view of the output neurons and only one convolutional layer at each resolution as shown in Fig. 2(right).

The first network takes a full data volume at a reduced resolution as an input and produces an estimate of the missing shape with the corresponding resolution. A laterally flipped copy of the volume is also concatenated to the input of this network to facilitate easier propagation of information from one side of the skull to the other [6]. The second network takes a single patch of the original resolution input concatenated to the up-sampled patch of the low-resolution estimate at the corresponding position and produces the final missing shape estimate in this patch. Both networks are trained using their respective resolution ground-truth. Each training step comprises of two updates. First, the low-resolution network weights are updated using the low-resolution ground-truth. Next, both low- and high-resolution networks weights are updated using the high-resolution ground-truth. The patches are chosen randomly during the training. Evaluating the second network using a window sliding over all the positions in the low-resolution estimate produces the full missing shape at the original resolution.

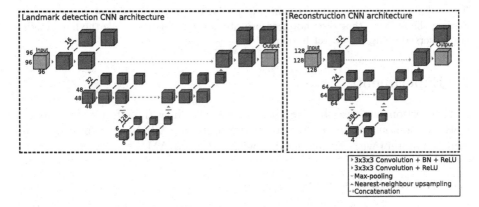

Fig. 2. Architectures of the 3D CNN models used for landmark detection (left) and shape reconstruction (right).

The architecture of both of the reconstruction networks is shown in Fig. 2(right) and the training details can be found in Sect. 3. The reconstruction model is described in further detail by Kodym et al. [6].

2.3 Shape Post-Processing

The reconstruction model will occasionally produce outputs that contain noise, such as disjoint objects or protuberances covering the healthy part of the skull as shown in Fig. 3(left). We make an assumption that the missing shapes should only consist of a single compact object. First, to isolate only the main missing shape, we use connected component analysis and discard all objects except the largest one. Second, we use morphological opening operation to remove any shape protuberances with less than desired minimum shape thickness.

However, the opening operation also tends to produce overly smooth shapes along the defect edges where it is desirable to keep the fine details produced by the reconstruction model. To address this, we keep both the original and morphologically open shapes. We then apply an additional morphological dilation to the open shape, producing a mask that is slightly bigger than the original shape but does not include the protuberances. Masking the original shape with such a mask results in a shape with the original fine details but without the larger protuberances as shown in Fig. 3(right).

Fig. 3. Example of the detail-preserving morphological post-processing of the estimated missing shape. Note that the undesired protuberance is removed while the fine details are preserved along the object border.

3   Experiments

In this section, we describe the experiments and show the effect of individual method components on the reconstruction outputs. All the experiments were run on a system with Titan Xp GPU with 12 GB GRAM.

3.1   Landmark Detection

We manually annotated the four landmarks in all 100 training skull volumes. We trained the landmark detection CNN model on 90 samples, leaving 10 skulls for validation. The model was trained for 100 000 iterations using Adam optimizer with training step 10^{-4} and the dataset was strongly augmented using random rotations to ascertain that the model is able to detect the landmarks in cases of arbitrary patient positions inside the scanner.

The results of the landmark detection on the 10 validation cases can be seen in Fig. 4(left). The auditory meatus landmarks were detected with error of 1.22 ± 0.70 mm while the supraorbital notch landmarks achieved a slightly higher error of 1.84 ± 1.03 mm. An important observation is that the trained model also succeeded in detection of all four landmarks in all the 110 testing cases as well, and every skull could be aligned fully automatically without any manual intervention at test time.

3.2   Missing Shape Inference

Similarly to the landmark detection model, the reconstruction networks were also trained on 90 training samples. For the ablation experiments in this work, both low- and high-resolution networks were trained on batches of 4 samples using Adam optimizer with training step 10^{-4} for 50 000 iterations using resolution of 3.2 mm per voxel and 0.4 mm per voxel, respectively. All data volumes were padded to dimensions $512 \times 512 \times 512$ which means that the corresponding low-resolution samples had dimensions $64 \times 64 \times 64$. Random lateral flips were used to augment the dataset.

We trained three different reconstruction models. The *basic cascade model* is trained on the original provided challenge data. The mirrored input channel is not used in the low-resolution network of this model as the sagittal plane is not known. The *aligned model* is trained on the data that have been previously aligned using the detected landmark positions. This also allows us to use the mirrored channel in this model. The *aligned and augmented* model is also trained on additional defective skulls that have been created from the training complete skulls. Five defects were created on each skull using random shapes similarly to the SkullBreak dataset, resulting in additional 450 training cases. We also created 10 additional validation cases using the same process.

The results of the reconstruction model on the validation cases are shown in Fig. 4(right). The basic cascade model had the worst performance on the validation cases, achieving average Dice score of 0.835. Simply aligning the data and adding the mirrored input to the low-resolution network in the aligned model had a substantial effect on the model performance, reaching 0.895 Dice score and showing the benefit of reducing the degrees of freedom of the defects during the reconstruction. However, both models overfit strongly to the training dataset with specific shape and position of the defects and were unable to generalize to the additional augmented validation cases where the distribution of defect shapes and positions is different. The aligned and augmented model trained on the additional defective cases, on the other hand, was able to both reconstruct the additional validation cases and increase the original data accuracy to Dice score 0.903.

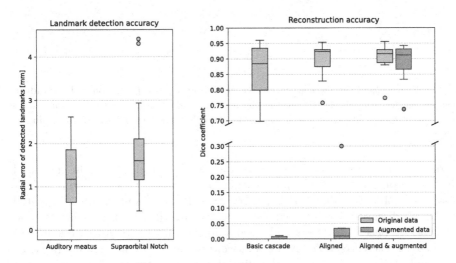

Fig. 4. Accuracy of the landmark detection (left) and the reconstruction models (right) on the validation cases.

4   Results

We aligned both subsets of the final 110 test cases of the AutoImplant challenge using the landmark detection model. For reconstruction, we used the aligned and

Table 1. The results of the proposed method on the AutoImplant Challenge test dataset in terms of Dice score and Hausdorff distance.

	Test case (100)	Test case (10)	Overall (110)
Mean DSC	0.920	0.910	0.919
Mean HD	4.137	4.707	4.189

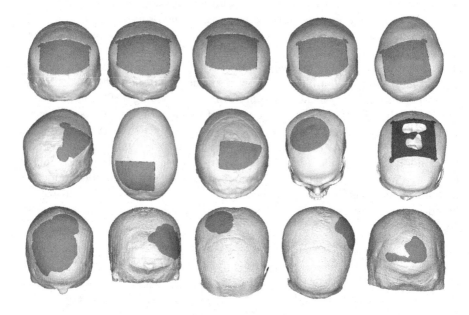

Fig. 5. Examples of the reconstruction results. From top row to bottom: The standard test set, the additional test set and the augmented validation set. Reconstruction failure could be observed in the last case of the additional test set in red color. (Color figure online)

augmented model that had been trained for 120 000 iterations. We also increased the first reconstruction network resolution to 1.6 mm per voxel, resulting in low-resolution volumes of dimensions 128 × 128 × 128 voxels in the final evaluated model. To discard the occasional artifacts, we used the post-processing method described in Sect. 2.3. Both standard and additional subsets of the test dataset were reconstructed completely automatically without any manual interactions. The landmark detection model, the aligned training dataset and the augmented training dataset are publicly available[1].

The results of the proposed method on the challenge test dataset in terms of Dice coefficient and Hausdorff distance are shown in Table 1. Several qualitative examples of the reconstruction output on the standard subset, the additional subset and also the augmented validation dataset are shown in Fig. 5 where one case of reconstruction failure on the additional test set can also be observed.

---

[1] https://github.com/OldaKodym/BUT_autoimplant_public.

5   Conclusion

Our experiments showed that the skull alignment and data augmentation techniques we used increase the accuracy of the skull reconstruction. These are general concepts that could be applied to any other reconstruction model. Although we only encountered one failure case in our experiments, it hints at the fact that more defect shape augmentations should be used to increase robustness of the reconstruction model. It is currently unknown whether the achieved accuracy in terms of Dice coefficient and Hausdorff distance could warrant clinical applicability of the method. However, visual inspection of the reconstructed defects shows no visible artifacts in most cases.

While the reconstruction method reaches good accuracy, the final shape will usually have to be further edited by an experienced clinician in medical practice. Therefore, it would be beneficial to explore ways to include interactivity in the implant design method, possibly drawing inspiration from interactive convolutional networks that have been successfully applied to segmentation tasks. Another interesting research direction is leveraging different data representations such point clouds or level sets.

Acknowledgements. This work was partly supported by TESCAN Medical and TESCAN 3DIM companies. We gratefully acknowledge the support of the NVIDIA Corporation with the donation of the NVIDIA TITAN Xp GPU for this research.

References

1. Besl, P., McKay, N.D.: A method for registration of 3-D shapes. IEEE Trans. Pattern Anal. Mach. Intell. **14**(2), 239–256 (1992). https://doi.org/10.1109/34. 121791
2. Chen, X., Xu, L., Li, X., Egger, J.: Computer-aided implant design for the restoration of cranial defects. Sci. Rep. **7**(1), 1–10 (2017). https://doi.org/10.1038/s41598-017-04454-6
3. Drevický, D., Kodym, O.: Evaluating deep learning uncertainty measures in cephalometric landmark localization. In: Proceedings of the 13th International Joint Conference on Biomedical Engineering Systems and Technologies. SCITEPRESS - Science and Technology Publications (2020). https://doi.org/10. 5220/0009375302130220
4. Fuessinger, M.A., et al.: Planning of skull reconstruction based on a statistical shape model combined with geometric morphometrics. Int. J. Comput. Assist. Radiol. Surg. **13**(4), 519–529 (2017). https://doi.org/10.1007/s11548-017-1674-6
5. Fuessinger, M.A., et al.: Virtual reconstruction of bilateral midfacial defects by using statistical shape modeling. J. Cranio-Maxillofac. Surg. **47**(7), 1054–1059 (2019). https://doi.org/10.1016/j.jcms.2019.03.027
6. Kodym, O., Španěl, M., Herout, A.: Skull shape reconstruction using cascaded convolutional networks. Comput. Biol. Med. **123**, 103886 (2020). https://doi.org/ 10.1016/j.compbiomed.2020.103886
7. Kurland, D.B., et al.: Complications associated with decompressive craniectomy: a systematic review. Neurocrit. Care **23**(2), 292–304 (2015). https://doi.org/10. 1007/s12028-015-0144-7

8. Lee, M.Y., Chang, C.C., Lin, C.C., Lo, L.J., Chen, Y.R.: Custom implant design for patients with cranial defects. IEEE Eng. Med. Biol. Mag. **21**(2), 38–44 (2002). https://doi.org/10.1109/MEMB.2002.1000184

9. Li, J., Pepe, A., Gsaxner, C., Campe, G., Egger, J.: A baseline approach for autoimplant: the MICCAI 2020 cranial implant design challenge. In: Syeda-Mahmood, T., et al. (eds.) CLIP/ML-CDS -2020. LNCS, vol. 12445, pp. 75–84. Springer, Cham (2020). https://doi.org/10.1007/978-3-030-60946-7_8

10. Li, J., Pepe, A., Gsaxner, C., Egger, J.: An online platform for automatic skull defect restoration and cranial implant design (2020)

11. Matzkin, F., et al.: Self-supervised skull reconstruction in brain CT images with decompressive craniectomy. In: Martel, A.L., et al. (eds.) MICCAI 2020. LNCS, vol. 12262, pp. 390–399. Springer, Cham (2020). https://doi.org/10.1007/978-3-030-59713-9_38

12. Morais, A., Egger, J., Alves, V.: Automated computer-aided design of cranial implants using a deep volumetric convolutional denoising autoencoder. In: Rocha, Á., Adeli, H., Reis, L.P., Costanzo, S. (eds.) WorldCIST'19 2019. AISC, vol. 932, pp. 151–160. Springer, Cham (2019). https://doi.org/10.1007/978-3-030-16187-3_15

13. Payer, C., Štern, D., Bischof, H., Urschler, M.: Regressing heatmaps for multiple landmark localization using CNNs. In: Ourselin, S., Joskowicz, L., Sabuncu, M.R., Unal, G., Wells, W. (eds.) MICCAI 2016. LNCS, vol. 9901, pp. 230–238. Springer, Cham (2016). https://doi.org/10.1007/978-3-319-46723-8_27

Shape Completion by U-Net: An Approach to the AutoImplant MICCAI Cranial Implant Design Challenge

James G. Mainprize[1,2](✉) ⓘ, Zachary Fishman[1] ⓘ, and Michael R. Hardisty[1,3] ⓘ

[1] Sunnybrook Research Institute, 2075 Bayview Avenue, Toronto, ON, Canada
james.mainprize@sri.utoronto.ca
[2] Calavera Surgical Design Inc., Toronto, ON, Canada
[3] Division of Orthopaedic Surgery, University of Toronto, Toronto, ON, Canada

Abstract. Reconstruction of the craniomaxillofacial (CMF) skeleton requires patient specific implants that restore cosmesis and protect the neural structures. Designing 3D patient specific geometries is challenging and labor intensive because of the lack of pre-injury information. We present an automated shape completion framework for the MICCAI AutoImplant Challenge 2020. The automated workflow selected standardized segmented skull volumes from the skull base to the apex. A U-Net style encoder/decoder framework was used to create the predictive model. The training data consisted of defective skulls with matched intact skulls. The challenge training set (100 cases) was augmented by randomly placed cubic and spherical defects on the same 100 cases for a total of 300 samples split 75/25% by case into a training and validation set. Probability volumes of the predicted skulls were generated by the U-Net and segmented to create an intact skull. Subtraction with defect skulls was used to isolate the implant geometry and were denoised with a connected region extraction of the single largest object, followed by a spherical topological filter. Dice Score (DSC) was 0.86 and Hausdorff distance (HD) was 14.2 mm for the validation set of 25 skulls (×3 defect types). Filtering improved the predicted implants with DSC of 0.87 and HD of 6.72. The automated pipeline for generating implants, produced geometries suitable for integration into a clinical pipeline that could dramatically decrease design time, cost, and increase reconstruction accuracy.

Keywords: Craniofacial surgery · Deep learning · Patient-specific implants

1 Introduction

The craniomaxillofacial (CMF) skeleton forms a complex three-dimensional (3D) structure that is important to both function and psychosocial well-being. CMF trauma and pathologic disease deformity can result in major disruption of skeletal integrity, with extensive loss of bone. Reconstructions of established deformities are compromised by insufficient patient-specific information of prior 3D face shape and skeletal anatomy.

© Springer Nature Switzerland AG 2020
J. Li and J. Egger (Eds.): AutoImplant 2020, LNCS 12439, pp. 65–76, 2020.
https://doi.org/10.1007/978-3-030-64327-0_8

Under these circumstances, accurate restoration of premorbid appearance is challenging, as the geometry of the facial structures needed to guide surgical planning and reconstruction are unavailable.

If a pre-op CT dataset is available and covers the complete skull, implant design following craniotomy is trivial. However, in most cases of head trauma, the defect has already occurred before the CT is taken. Localized unilateral defects can be corrected by mirroring the skull from the unaffected side, either automatically, or with minimal manual effort. For larger, bilateral defects, the process becomes more complicated. Designed by hand, this may require several hours of design by an experienced user.

Automated methods for predicting the skull shape would therefore be extremely useful in removing the guesswork and dramatically reducing design times. The MICCAI AutoImplant Challenge 2020 formulated the problem of automated implant design as a shape completion problem. This formulation of the problem allows training and evaluation of implant generation algorithms to be possible from datasets of otherwise normal skull geometry that may be available from medical imaging repositories including those for CT angiography, brain tumour diagnosis and treatment. In the Challenge, the implants are synthetically created on a bony segmented CT scan such that both the truth (either the intact skull or implant piece) and the defect skull are available.

This investigation focused on using a deep learning-based approach to perform this shape completion task. Deep models, CNNs and in particular the U-Net have been shown to be able to model many complex functions and have motivated their use for a variety of tasks, including, segmentation, registration, filtering medical image as well as modelling physical processes [1, 2]. The receptive fields of the features learned within most U-Net designs in the literature are sufficient to describe object shape and texture, with deeper features being related to larger shapes and shallower features related to texture and allowing finer details to be modeled [3].

Statistical shape models (SSM) have been applied extensively in the literature to the various craniofacial reconstruction problems with good results [4–6]. For example, Fuessinger *et al.* [6] reported HD values of 2.22 mm. Cranial reconstruction has also been planned indirectly using head shape models, rather than directly from the skull shape from the Headspace database (consisting of ~1500 subjects) [4]. However, this investigation did not pursue an SSM because of our intent to continue development of this method and make use of open datasets and datasets within our institution to improve robustness and performance. Deep learning methods can derive improvements from large datasets that cannot be achieved by other methods.

2 Methods

This investigation presents an automated workflow for implant generation within the cranium (Fig. 1). The workflow takes as input binary segmented skull volumes with defects and generates implant volumes suitable for reconstructing the defects. The approach as described below involves cropping and rescaling the input volumes, inference of the whole intact skull volume with a U-Net, subtraction of the original skull with defect volume and post-processing (filtering and denoising).

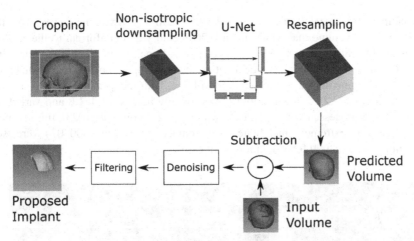

Fig. 1. Workflow for generating an implant from a defect skull.

2.1 Dataset

The training dataset provided as part of the MICCAI AutoImplant grand challenge consisted of 100 binary (bone = 1) segmented skull volumes at various fields of view, slice spacing and head positioning. Coverage generally went from the skull base to the apex, although several include most of the maxilla and several included coverages to the mandible and portions of the neck. Volumes were $512 \times 512 \times Z$ where Z slices range from 150–300. In-plane and slice spacing were variable across the dataset.

2.2 Preprocessing

Typically, there is a large air volume around the skull in a head CT (to ensure that no anatomic regions are clipped). Also, the skull is generally much narrower along the lateral aspect (ear to ear) than anterior-posterior (A/P) direction, such that the skull usually only occupies a region approximately 380×500 (axial) at its greatest extent. As a result, there is a significant amount of "wasted" voxels that provide no information. As well, volumes that included extra anatomy below the midface that is unnecessary for the given task (upper skull craniotomy restoration).

Healthy skulls have a high degree of homology (anatomic features look similar) regardless of the size of the skull [7]. Thus, it may be beneficial to remove size variability in the dataset by rescaling the skulls to a common size.

The skull CTs were preprocessed by first cropping the original volume to a useful region defined by a bounding box enclosing all non-zero voxels in the x and y directions. In the z-direction, the cropping was identified from the skull apex to approximately the skull base. The skull base was identified by a matrix summation along the x and y directions to create a projection vector along z. The location corresponding to the peak projection is assumed to be the most bone which nearly always corresponds to a line through the skull base. The cropping volume was given an additional clear boundary of 8 voxels in each direction to avoid clipping of the bone. All volumes were then downsampled and rescaled into a standard $192 \times 256 \times 128$ volume representing the largest practical volume that would fit in GPU memory and conformal to the relative dimensions (Medial-Lateral $\times$ Anterior-Posterior $\times$ Superior-Inferior) of the bounding boxes containing the cranium. The data within the cropping volume were rescaled non-isotropically to maximally fit the standard volume, with independent scaling in each direction. Nominal "2×" downsampling was roughly between 1.4–1.8 and varied for each skull. Pre-processed volumes are shown in Fig. 2. In one case (023), this estimate failed, because of extremely thick bone in the frontal cortex). Skulls 000–074 were used for training and 075–099 for validation in all cases.

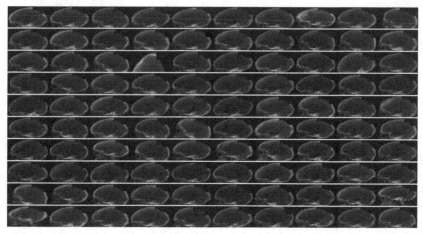

Fig. 2. Digitally reconstructed radiographs (sagittal) of the training set of original defect skulls (000–099 ordered from top left) after rescaling to a standard volume. The cropping algorithm partially failed on 023 but was still included in the training. Skulls 075–099 were reserved for validation for all runs.

From Fig. 2, it is apparent that nearly all the implants are localized generally to the skull posterior and nearly identical shape. To improve generalization, two additional sets of training/validation data were generated by creating cubic and spherical defects on the same skulls. This was created based on defect injection code originally provided in the challenge code base [8]. The code was modified to allow for random locations anywhere on the skull above the horizontal midplane. A valid defective skull was allowed if the defect removed at least 2% of the bony volume. The random defects were generated once for each skull and defect type (100 skulls with three defects: original, cubic, and spherical) and divided case-wise (same as original) into training/validation data,

The test sets consisted of the main data (test000–test099) as well as an additional set (test100–test109) that was provided for the AutoImplant Challenge. These test sets were processed in the same fashion as the training/validation sets. Upon submission, the calculated results by the organizers were returned to the authors.

2.3   U-Net for Shape Completion

The U-Net [2] scheme used here is illustrated in Fig. 1. This base configuration consists of 5 levels in the U-Net, with 8 filters for the first level and doubling for each successive level. Long skip connections from each down-level were concatenated to the corresponding up-level. Each convolutional block consisted of two 3D convolutional layers, both with (3, 3, 3) kernels followed by batch normalization, a "ReLu" activation layer and a MaxPooling layer. The bottom (bottleneck) block consisted of two convolutional layers (32 filters), batch normalization and ReLu activation. The up levels consisted of a 3D transpose convolutional layer, skip concatenation and convolutional block. A softmax output layer is used to generate 3D voxel prediction.

Training used an Adam optimizer. Learning rate began at 10^{-3} and was reduced by 20% if the validation loss did not improve for two epochs. We used 1-Dice Similarity as the loss function. Batch size was limited to a single skull volume, and an epoch was set to 150 randomly selected samples from the 225 skulls (75 unique skulls $\times$ 3 defect types). Image augmentation was performed with randomized small lateral and anterior-posterior shifts ($-2,2$ voxels), rotations in the axial plane (5), and mirroring (left-right) of the skull volumes. Up to 30 epochs were allowed, which were terminated early if 10 epochs occurred with no improvement in the loss.

The algorithm was coded in Python (3.7.7), with the keras-gpu 2.4.3 and tensorflow-gpu 2.2.0 modules, and inspired by "UNET-Conv3D Baseline" [9] and "Keras U-Net" [10]. Training and analysis were run on a 3.8 GHz AMD Ryzen 2600 processor (6 cores) 32 GB RAM, with a GeForce GTX 1660Ti (6 GB) GPU in Ubuntu 18.04.

Alternative Networks: To test alternative network schemes, networks were retrained and evaluated by 1) swapping the bottleneck with a two simple dense layers (64 units each), and 2) changing from "2$\times$" downsampling to either: 'full' isotropic "1$\times$" resolution at 320 $\times$ 448 $\times$ 192 (resampling from roughly 0.8$\times$ to 1.2$\times$) or "4$\times$" at 96 $\times$ 128 $\times$ 64, (resampling roughly 2.75$\times$ to 4.2$\times$ downsampling depending on the axis for each skull).

2.4   Post-processing

Predictions from the U-Net were resampled onto the original skull bounding box and then to the original image grid. An implant bounding box was estimated by subtracting a morphologically dilated defective skull from the prediction to mask out unneeded bone and determining the box containing the implant by thresholding voxels greater than 0.6. An exclusion zone of the first 10 slices near the skull base was also used to avoid catching problematic noisy predictions in that region. In the bounding box, the implant was calculated by thresholding the model prediction to 0.5 and subtracting the original defective skull. Random small noisy objects were excluded using the "connected components 3d" (pypi.org/project/connected-components-3d/) module that extracts and labels binary connected objects – based on code provided in the original AutoImplant Challenge repository [8]. Within the challenge, defects were confined to the cranium. As such, we assumed spherical topology and smooth bony prominences. A post-processing spherical topological filter [11] was applied in 3D Slicer (www.slicer.org). Interior holes were filled, and the label map was smoothed with binary closing and a level set based anti-aliasing filter.

2.5 Analysis

The generated implants were compared to truth for the validation set. The average relative volume (Predicted Volume/Actual Volume), Dice Similarity Coefficient (DSC) and Hausdorff Distance (HD) were reported for each defect type (original, cubic, spherical) as well as the 90% interpercentile range (IPR) from 5th to 95th percentile of measured values, reported in brackets as "$[x_{5th}-x_{95th}]$". All calculations after training were performed at the original resolution.

Fig. 3. Outlines of the predicted implant before (left) and after (right) post-processing by the topological filter. The thin finger artifacts are removed, without loss of the main implant.

3 Results

The best results achieved by the workflow were with the $2\times$ downsampled U-Net for the validation, test, and challenge sets. Training resulted in a dice loss of 0.038, binary accuracy 0.963 and mean-square error (MSE) of 0.0031 calculated on the whole skull for the $192 \times 256 \times 128$ volumes. Dice loss was minimized after 19 epochs, with more epochs not reducing loss, with training history curves confirming a plateau. Validation dice loss was 0.006, binary accuracy 0.999 and MSE was 0.0013. Training values were slightly worse than the validation set, likely because augmentation was only used on the training data, and greater variation in skull poses (and the poorly cropped case 023).

Following post-processing, the relative volume, DSC, and HD were reported in Table 1 for the network analyzed at original resolution and voxel dimensions. Adding the post-processing step of the spherical topological filter had a small effect on the DSC, but a dramatic effect on the HD (Table 2), with 60% reduction for all implants. This step tended to remove thin fingerlike extensions (Fig. 3) that are an artifact of slight errors introduced by the downsampling and resampling steps. The failing spherical implant 090 was included in the results in Tables 1 and 2. If omitted, the values in Table 2 would improve to DSC 0.86 (+0.04) and HD 4.75 mm (−6.81) for the spherical implants, consistent with the other defect types.

Examples of good predictions for the three defect types are shown in Fig. 4. The sphere defects had the poorest predictions, especially for frontal defects (Fig. 5 and

Fig. 6) Some of the cubic implants fared poorly when they were located more laterally (near the ear). This may be partly due to an under representation of exemplar cases in the training set for the frontal and lateral regions. Of note, for the original defect, case 085 (Fig. 5 left), the implant appears to be qualitatively good except for the lower left margin where the prediction fails to capture the asymmetry in the original skull (most noticeable by comparing the left and right sides around the occipital lobe).

Figure 8 shows examples of the implants predicted for the challenge test set. Table 3 lists the test set results, with good performance on the main set (DSC 0.907 and HD 4.18 mm) and only slightly less well on the more difficult set (DSC 0.87 and HD 4.75 mm). The authors note one failure (DSC 0.61) on test009 that could be fixed

Table 1. Relative volume, Dice score and Hausdorff distance (HD, in mm) for the validation set (075–099), tested on the original, cubic, and spherical simulated skull defect shapes.

	Relative volume			Dice score			HD		
	Mean	[5th–95th]*	IPR*	Mean	[5th–95th]	IPR	Mean	[5th–95th]	IPR
Original	1.02	[0.93–1.13]	0.20	0.91	[0.86–0.94]	0.09	12.45	[8.3–34.8]	26.49
Cubic	1.07	[0.84–1.37]	0.53	0.86	[0.7–0.9]	0.18	11.15	[5.–37.7]	32.71
Sphere	0.88	[0.55–1.08]	0.54	0.82	[0.9–0.9]	0.31	18.87	[9.1–49.2]	40.10
Overall	**0.99**	**[0.77–1.25]**	**0.48**	**0.86**	**[0.7–0.9]**	**0.25**	**14.16**	**[5.2–42.4]**	**37.25**

*Values at the 5th and 95th percentile. Interpercentile Range (IPR) is the difference between 95th and 5th percentile in the data.

Table 2. Relative volume, Dice score and Hausdorff distance (HD) for the validation set after filtering (cases 075–099).

	Relative volume			Dice score			HD		
	Mean	[5th–95th]*	IPR*	Mean	[5th–95th]	IPR	Mean	[5th–95th]	IPR
Original	1.02	[0.93–1.13]	0.20	0.91	[0.86–0.94]	0.09	3.64	[2.43–6.01]	3.58
Cubic	1.06	[0.83–1.33]	0.50	0.86	[0.75–0.93]	0.18	4.95	[2.35–8.62]	6.27
Sphere	0.87	[0.54–1.07]	0.53	0.82	[0.63–0.94]	0.31	11.56	[2.1–11.91]	9.81
Overall	**0.98**	**[0.76–1.24]**	**0.76**	**0.87**	**[0.69–0.94]**	**0.25**	**6.72**	**[2.17–10.2]**	**8.03**

Table 3. Summary of DSC and HD for the test set submission

Cases	DSC	HD (mm)
test000-test099	0.907 [0.856–0.945]	4.18 [2.65–6.75]
test100-test109	0.87 [0.707–0938]	4.76 [2.68–8.92]
test000-test109 (combined)	0.904 [0.842–0.943]	4.23 [2.60–7.25]

by manually selecting the skull base for preprocessing. In the spirit of "fully automatic processing", we left the case as is.

Alternative Networks: The bottleneck was replaced with a block consisting of two fully connected dense layers (64 units each) which reduced the number of trainable weights from 6,486,939 to 3,931,035. On the original and cubic defects, the dense-layer bottleneck performed better within the validation set, with a modest improvement in DSC (0.85 [0.78–0.91]) and dramatic improvement in HD (10.2 mm [8.3–10.0]) NB: a few outliers greatly skewed the average in HD. However, the sphere defects had a DSC worsened by −0.036 with only a modest improvement in HD (−2.2 mm). Although it did not perform better overall, it does suggest further optimization is possible with more streamlined networks.

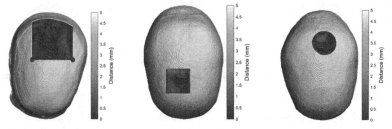

Fig. 4. Examples of well predicted implants. Colourmaps correspond to the shortest distance (in mm) from the implant surface to the target (truth) surface. Left is an original defect (case 080 DSC 0.95), centre is a cubic defect (case 099 DSC 0.94), and right is a spherical defect (case 084 DSC 0.97).

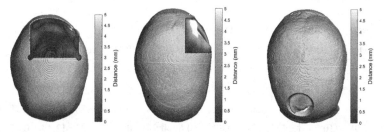

Fig. 5. Examples of poorly predicted implants. Left is an original defect (case 085 DSC 0.74), centre is a cubic defect (case 091 DSC 0.66) and right is a spherical defect (case 094 DSC 0.51).

Using the smaller input volume ("4×" downsampling), training epoch times were reduced from 496 to 29 s. On the validation set, the implants generated from the "4×" set, the mean DSC was 0.865 [0.73–0.933] and mean HD was 5.8 [2.52–9.44] which are nearly unchanged from the "2×" set. However, visual inspection (Fig. 7) reveals strong terracing artifacts that are not captured by either DSC or HD metrics. Correspondingly, larger input volume ("1×") were also considered and trained on a server with 128 GB and RTX Titans with 24 GB GPU RAM. Training was confined to a single card and

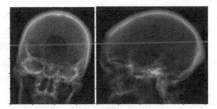

Fig. 6. The sphere defect for case 090 was entirely on the forehead bisecting the sinuses. Only a tiny implant was predicted (<1% volume), not shown. More of the maxilla and mandible are included than other cases, and head pose is significantly tilted laterally.

Fig. 7. Comparison surface renders (marching cubes) of the desired implant (left), the predicted implant from the "2×" downsampled data (middle, DSC 0.92), and "4×" data (right, DSC 0.93) for validation case 083. Note that, despite the slightly improved DSC, the "4×" is a decidedly inferior result because of noticeable terracing.

epoch training times were larger, at 1156 s, making hyper-parameter optimization of the model impractical. Higher resolution did not improve results in the validation set with DSC = 0.751 [0–92.8], HD = 12.0 mm [2.26–161.68].

4   Discussion

This investigation presented a U-Net solution to the MICCAI AutoImplant grand challenge with performance suitable for use in a clinical design pipeline. The pipeline achieved average results of DSC = 0.90 and HD = 4.23 mm, with one failed implant. This accuracy is likely sufficient for use clinically with appropriate verification and post-processing. The algorithm has the potential to drastically reduce design times to minutes, for the creation of patient-specific implants for craniofacial surgery, the algorithm requires no user input other than to supply the initial segmentation.

The implants generated at higher resolutions were qualitatively smooth and restored cosmesis. The errors of the generated implant designed by the algorithm within this investigation were of a similar magnitude to other potential sources of error when reconstructing the defect in the cranium surgically. Placement of instrumentation by trained surgeons has been measured as 1–2 mm with indexing and navigation reducing placement errors to 0.5–1 mm [12].

Quantitative analysis was limited to relative volume, DSC, and HD. However, important considerations related to the clinical need for these implants were not considered, such as minimizing discontinuities at the defect boundaries, ensuring that the inner boundary does not impinge on the brain, and that the outer surface must be smooth.

The HD values were often a result of errors in implant thickness or errors in the implant curvature. Skull thickness range from 3–14 mm and change in curvature may still allow for adequate cosmetic restoration depending on the site of reconstruction [13].

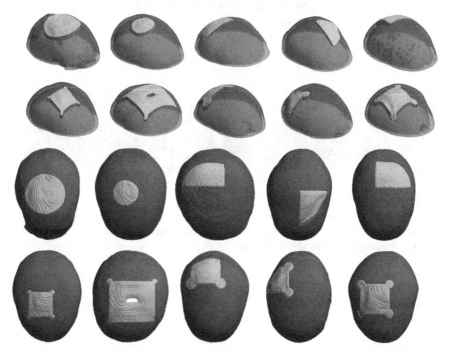

Fig. 8. Examples of the "Additional" cases (test100-test109) in the challenge set in isometric view (top two rows) and top view (bottom two rows). Note that these cases were deemed as challenging by the organizers and that the ideal geometry was withheld by the challenge organizers.

The dataset used in this Grand Challenge was derived from 100 head CT volumes taken from ~500 scans publicly provided by Qure AI (qure.ai/headct.html) With other open databases, such as the SICAS Medical Image Repository (www.smir.ch) or Cancer Imaging Archive (www.cancerimagingarchive.net), containing hundreds of subjects that could be used to improve the performance of deep models. Furthermore, institutions likely have access to orders of magnitude more skull CT scans than are available publicly, potentially allowing for dramatic improvements in performance.

There are many limitations of the approach investigated here. Specifically, the variability of the data considered was quite limited, differences in pose, resolution, scan image quality, and gantry tilt would all likely have an impact on the accuracy of the results. The model may, therefore, not generalize well. Limited tests of the robustness of the networks showed that errors in the cropping of the validation and test data led to large changes in performance. This is consistent with the literature that showed differences in image quality derived from changes in imaging hardware have been demonstrated to have significant effects on image processing. Further, our results showed differences in performance with the respect to defect shape. These known effects (image and defect variation) could be addressed by suitable data augmentation strategies [14] and by network architectures designed to address these issues [15].

Reorienting the skull into a standard pose (*e.g.*, aligning to a craniometric Frankfort horizontal plane) may reduce pose-dependent variability. Similarly, shape standardization by a Procrustes method [16] or by 3D registration, may also reduce variability over the crude cropping and scaling approach used here. At least one training sample (023) and, likely, one test case (test009), were incorrectly oriented.

The trained network is likely limited to single defects following craniotomy, with the training data drawn from an adult population. Restoration of congenital defects, or restoration of symmetry beyond simple 'hole filling' is likely beyond the scope of the network. Pediatric skull shapes have not been explored in this current work. Nevertheless, given the robust, scalable, modifiable nature of the U-Net for shape completion, future work could explore including pediatric skull training data and applying these techniques to congenital skull malformations (*e.g.* craniosynostosis) [4, 17].

Finally, generation of the predicted bone is but the first step in the design. The addition of holes for drainage and fixation, tabs to secure the implant to the surface, and modification of the shape for areas of difficult access, are all expected steps which may benefit from automation as well.

5 Conclusion

The proposed processing pipeline was shown to robustly generate implants with high accuracy and visually acceptable cosmesis in a time-efficient manner by training a U-Net architecture to predict implant shapes from the defective skull. The algorithms developed within this investigation will be integrated within a comprehensive implant generation framework, allowing engineers and surgeons to quickly design patient specific implants, dramatically reducing design time from hours to minutes.

With greater public data available the approach taken in this investigation will find new application, perhaps to the mandible and will further improve in robustness and performance. Future work could extend the algorithm implemented here to other indications, including congenital defects, pediatric reconstructions. Further these methods could incorporate the use of patient-specific factors, such as sex, age, or ethnicity, by introducing meta-data within dense layers at the bottleneck to augment latent variables within the network, as well as generating bespoke skull shape training data-sets by sorting according to this meta-data and oversampling these under represented geometries.

References

1. He, S., et al.: Learning to predict the cosmological structure formation. Proc. Natl. Acad. Sci. **116**(28), 13825–13832 (2019). 201821458
2. Ronneberger, O., Fischer, P., Brox, T.: U-Net: convolutional networks for biomedical image segmentation. In: Navab, N., Hornegger, J., Wells, W.M., Frangi, A.F. (eds.) MICCAI 2015. LNCS, vol. 9351, pp. 234–241. Springer, Cham (2015). https://doi.org/10.1007/978-3-319-24574-4_28

3. Geirhos, R., Rubisch, P., Michaelis, C., Bethge, M., Wichmann, F.A., Brendel, W.: ImageNet-trained CNNs are biased towards texture; increasing shape bias improves accuracy and robustness, pp. 1–22 (2018)

4. Dai, H., Pears, N., Duncan, C.: Modelling of orthogonal craniofacial profiles. J. Imaging **3**, 55 (2017). https://doi.org/10.3390/jimaging3040055

5. Bruynooghe, E., Keustermans, J., Smeets, D., Tilotta, F., Claes, P., Vandermeulen, D.: CT-based robust statistical shape modeling for forensic craniofacial reconstruction. In: 4th International Conference on Imaging Crime Detection and Prevention 2011 (ICDP 2011), pp. 29–34 (2011). https://doi.org/10.1049/ic.2011.0126

6. Fuessinger, M.A., et al.: Planning of skull reconstruction based on a statistical shape model combined with geometric morphometrics. Int. J. Comput. Assist. Radiol. Surg. **13**(4), 519–529 (2017). https://doi.org/10.1007/s11548-017-1674-6

7. Pahuta, M.A., Mainprize, J.G., Rohlf, F.J., Antonyshyn, O.M.: Biometric morphing: a novel technique for the analysis of morphologic outcomes after facial surgery. Ann. Plast. Surg. **62**, 48–53 (2009). https://doi.org/10.1097/SAP.0b013e3181743386

8. Li, J., Pepe, A., Gsaxner, C., von Campe, G., Egger, J.: A baseline approach for autoimplant: the MICCAI 2020 cranial implant design challenge, pp. 1–12 (2020)

9. Mader, K.S.: UNET-Conv3D Baseline. www.kaggle.com/kmader/unet-conv3d-baseline. Accessed 10 Aug 2020

10. Żak, K.: Keras U-Net v.0.1.2, http://github.com/karolzak/keras-unet. Accessed 10 Aug 2020

11. Styner, M., et al.: Framework for the statistical shape analysis of brain structures using SPHARM-PDM. Insight J. 242–250 (2006)

12. Katsoulis, J., Katsoulis, K.: Accuracy of free hand vs pilot drill and fully guided oral implant placement. Clin. Oral Implants Res. **28**, 453 (2017). https://doi.org/10.1111/clr.450_13042

13. Mahinda, H.A.M., Murty, O.P.: Variability in thickness of human skull bones and sternum - an autopsy experience. J. Forensic Med. Toxicol. **26**, 26–31 (2009)

14. Klein, G., Hardisty, M., Sahgal, A., Whyne, C., Martel, A.: Vertebral body segmentation in CT images using V-Net. In: Imaging Network of Ontario, p. 29 (2019)

15. Jaderberg, M., Simonyan, K., Zisserman, A., Kavukcuoglu, K.: Spatial transformer networks. In: Advances in Neural Information Processing Systems, pp. 2017–2025 (2015)

16. Benazzi, S., Senck, S.: Comparing 3-dimensional virtual methods for reconstruction in craniomaxillofacial surgery. J. Oral Maxillofac. Surg. **69**, 1184–1194 (2011). https://doi.org/10.1016/j.joms.2010.02.028

17. Saber, N.R., et al.: Generation of normative pediatric skull models for use in cranial vault remodeling procedures. Child's Nerv. Syst. **28**, 405–410 (2012). https://doi.org/10.1007/s00381-011-1630-7

Cranial Implant Prediction Using Low-Resolution 3D Shape Completion and High-Resolution 2D Refinement

Amirhossein Bayat[1,2,3]([⊠]), Suprosanna Shit[1,3], Adrian Kilian[4],
Jürgen T. Liechtenstein[4], Jan S. Kirschke[2,3], and Bjoern H. Menze[1,3]

[1] Department of Informatics, Technical University of Munich, Munich, Germany
amir.bayat@tum.de
[2] Department of Neuroradiology, Klinikum rechts der Isar, Munich, Germany
[3] TranslaTUM Center for Translational Cancer Research, Munich, Germany
[4] Department for Oral and Maxillofacial Surgery,
University Hospital Schleswig-Holstein, Campus Kiel, Arnold-Heller-Strasse 3,
24105 Kiel, Germany

Abstract. Designing of a cranial implant needs a 3D understanding of the complete skull shape. Thus, taking a 2D approach is sub-optimal, since a 2D model lacks a holistic 3D view of both the defective and healthy skulls. Further, loading the whole 3D skull shapes at its original image resolution is not feasible in commonly available GPUs. To mitigate these issues, we propose a fully convolutional network composed of two subnetworks. The first subnetwork is designed to complete the shape of the downsampled defective skull. The second subnetwork upsamples the reconstructed shape slice-wise. We train both the 3D and 2D networks in tandem in an end-to-end fashion, with a hierarchical loss function. Our proposed solution accurately predicts a high-resolution 3D implant in the challenge test case in terms of dice-score and the Hausdorff distance.

Keywords: Cranial-implant design · Shape completion · 3D reconstruction · Super resolution

1 Introduction

Cranial implant design is a crucial task for clinical planning of cranioplasty [13]. Previous works mainly rely on freely available CAD tools for cranial implant design [4,6,8,14]. The time requirements and need for expert intervention for these approaches are a major hindrance for fast and in-prompt deployment. The AutoImplant challenge aims to look for simple and easy-to-use automatic solution that can accurately predict cranial implants. Keeping this in mind, we tailor our proposed solution to best fit the requirements of clinicians.

Previous literature [1] tend to exploit the geometric symmetry and predict cranial implant based on the unaffected skull region. Nevertheless, this results

© Springer Nature Switzerland AG 2020
J. Li and J. Egger (Eds.): AutoImplant 2020, LNCS 12439, pp. 77–84, 2020.
https://doi.org/10.1007/978-3-030-64327-0_9

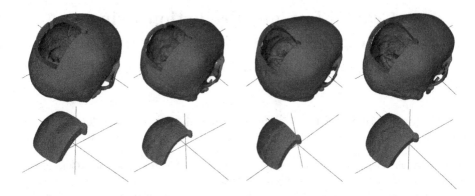

Fig. 1. Few training sample: The first row depicts rendered 3D volumes of four randomly selected defective scan from the training dataset. The second row shows the corresponding ground truth cranial implant.

in a suboptimal solution, since the human skull is not perfectly symmetric in reality. These solutions also fall short when the implant is not exclusively in one hemisphere. Morais et al. [15] used a deep 3D encoder-decoder [2,11,18] network to reconstruct the incomplete skull in low-resolution space. While the low-resolution space facilitates faster processing, the quality of the reconstruction lacks minute local anatomical detail. In the Autoimplant baseline paper [12], a similar approach is taken where the authors first localize the defective region in the skull and then predict the implant using an encoder-decoder network. While this pipeline is suitable for modular design of accurate defective region detection and implant prediction, the network is not end-to-end trainable, and thus any error during the first stages would penalize the implant prediction.

In this approach, we try to alleviate this by relying on coarse-scale implant prediction in 3D followed by fine-scale enhancement of the predicted implant. We identify that 3D is most suitable to predict the implant since anatomical consistency is best captured by a 3D receptive field compared to any local 2D slices. However, to reduce the memory and computational power, we first predict the implant in a down-sampled defective skull. Subsequently, we enhance the predicted implant slice wise by a 2D decoder network. Thus our solution becomes end-to-end trainable and also is efficient at the same time for the high-resolution implant prediction task.

2   Method

The dataset is created by artificially generating the defect in the scan [12]. Thus the original skull would be the ground truth for the implant prediction task. We leverage this availability of the target label and cast the implant prediction task as a supervised volumetric reconstruction task. At the core of our method lies a 3D encoder-decoder network. This network takes the low-resolution defective

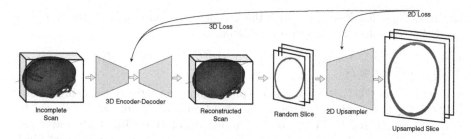

Fig. 2. Schematic overview of our proposed pipeline for predicting the cranial implant. The downsampled defective scan goes through an encoder-decoder based shape completion network. During training, N number of random reconstructed skull goes through a second decoder network for high-resolution reconstruction. For the 3D shape completion, we use a volumetric ℓ_1 norm, and for the 2D refinement task, we use summation of 2D ℓ_1 loss.

skull as input and predicts a low-resolution implant at the output. We argue that the implant prediction task lies in a lower-dimensional manifold since the key properties to predict implant are the inner and outer surface consistency. Hence, a down-sampled input space is sufficient for a coarse-scale identification of the implant region. A simple element-wise subtraction of the reconstructed skull and the input will produce the desired implant. This approach is in line with the shape completion literature [5,9,17,19,20]. Next, we need to upsample the predicted implant, which can be done in several ways. Classical approaches, such as spline-based interpolation, can be a simple choice. Alternatively, a decoder network proved to be superior in the super-resolution task [3,10]. Hence, we incorporate a second module in our method, a 2D up-sampler. This up-sampler takes selected axial slices during training and predicts the up-sampled version of it. To be able to train the both the network jointly and also fit the data in the GPU memory, we select N random slices out of the reconstructed shape and select the corresponding slices from the original scale Ground Truth. The error between the predicted slice and the ground truth skull is used to train the 2D decoder. The high-resolution reconstruction error, along with the 3D shape completion error, contributes to the training of the 3D encoder-decoder.

2.1 Network Architecture and Loss Function

In the following, we describe the architecture of two subnetworks in our model and the loss functions used to train the model.

3D Encoder-Decoder: Encoder-decoder type network has been previously used in bio-physical simulation [7], image segmentation [16] etc. Our 3D network has three sequential components, such as an encoder, bottleneck, and a decoder. The encoder further compresses the input signals into a more compact representation, which is processed in the bottleneck unit to extract useful features. These features go through the decoder part to reconstruct the complete skull. The complete architecture is as follows:

$$IN_1 \rightarrow CN_{64}^1 \rightarrow CN_{64}^2 \rightarrow CN_{64}^2 \rightarrow RB_{64} \rightarrow RB_{64} \rightarrow RB_{64} \rightarrow RB_{64} \rightarrow TC_{64}^2 \rightarrow$$
$$TC_{64}^2 \rightarrow C_1^1 \rightarrow OUT_1$$

where IN_1 and OUT_1 is input and output volume respectively with single channel, $CN_{\#ch}^s$ is convolution with stride s and output channel $\#ch$ followed by batch norm and ReLU, $TC_{\#ch}^s$ is transposed convolution with stride s and output channel $\#ch$ followed by batch norm and ReLU, $RB_{\#ch}$ is residual block consists of two successive unit of convolution with stride 1 and output channel $\#ch$ followed by instance norm and ReLU, and $C_{\#ch}^s$ is convolution with stride s and output channel $\#ch$ followed by sigmoid. Note that all convolution and norm layers described here are 3D.

2D Decoder Upsampler: The 2D upsampler network consists of four residual blocks, followed by the nearest neighborhood upsampling layer and a final convolution layer. The residual blocks refine the low-resolution reconstructed scans to incorporate anatomical consistency, which aids precise high-resolution skull at the output. We concatenate the corresponding slice of the defective scan along with the reconstructed scan and pass it as an input to the 2D upsampler. This helps to correct any location-wise mismatch in the 3D shape-completion task. Borrowing a few notations defined in the previous paragraph, the complete architecture is given below:

$$IN_2 \rightarrow CN_{64}^1 \rightarrow SE_{64} \rightarrow RB_{64} \rightarrow SE_{64} \rightarrow RB_{64} \rightarrow SE_{64} \rightarrow RB_{64} \rightarrow SE_{64} \rightarrow$$
$$RB_{64} \rightarrow NN_{64}^{sqrt(512/180)} \rightarrow NN_{64}^{sqrt(512/180)} \rightarrow C_1^1 \rightarrow OUT_1$$

where $SE\#ch$ is 'squeeze and excitation' layer and $NN_{\#ch}^s$ is Nearest Neighborhood (NN) upsample with scale factor s and output channel $\#ch$ followed by instance norm and ReLU. Note that all convolution and norm layers described here are 2D.

Loss Function: Let's denote the ground truth data at original scale as I_G, downsampled ground truth data I_g, defective 3D volume at original scale as I_D, downsampled defective 3D volume as I_d, the functional form of the 3D encoder-decoder network as $S()$, and the functional form of the 2D upsampler network as $U()$ respectively. The cranial implant is predicted as follows:

$$\text{Cranial Implant} = U(S(I_d)) \setminus I_D \tag{1}$$

where $\setminus$ denotes set difference. The total loss function of our method is as follows:

$$\mathcal{L}_{total} = \mathcal{L}_{3D} + \mathcal{L}_{2D} \tag{2}$$

$$\mathcal{L}_{3D} = \|S(I_d) - I_g\|_{\ell_1} \tag{3}$$

$$\mathcal{L}_{2D} = \sum_{i \in \Omega} \|U(S(I_d)^i) - I_G^i\|_{\ell_1} \tag{4}$$

where Ω is the set of random slices.

2.2 Implementation

We realize our model in PyTorch. We trained the networks with Adam optimizer and a learning rate of 0.0001. We used an Nvidia Quadro P6000 GPU. The batch size for the 3D network was 1, so one volume per iteration. **We downsampled the original 3D volume by a factor of $\frac{512}{180}$ in all dimension because that is the largest 3D volume we can fit in our GPU along with the 2D decoder module. The downsampled 3D volume is zero-padded in the z-dimension to make it** $180 \times 180 \times 180$. After predicting the completed 3D shape in low resolution, we sample 10 slices randomly along the Z-axis and concatenate them channel-wise with the downsampled corresponding slice from the defective skull and feed them to the upsampler decoder. We can't fit the entire volume with the original scale in the memory, so we have to select 2D slices. In order to avoid overfitting, we select the slices randomly. It is important to note that, after downsampling the volume with a $\frac{512}{180}$ scaling factor, every 3 slices along Z-axis in the original scale correspond to 1 slice in the downsampled volume. Thus, after reconstructing the 3D shape, we have a set of selected slices using random indices and three sets of [random indices/0.35], [random indices/0.35] + 1 and [random indices/0.35] + 2. We select the corresponding slices from the defective scan and downsample them in 2D to be concatenated with the slices from the predicted shape. Thus, the batch size for the upsampler decoder network is 30.

Inference: For inference, similarly, a downsampled volume is fed to the network, and it is reconstructed in low resolution using the first sub-network. After that, all of the slices along the Z-axis are fed to the upsampler decoder, one-by-one, and stacked in volume to reconstruct the shape in 3D. Subsequently, we subtract the defective input scan from the high-resolution reconstructed scans to estimate the cranial implant. Finally, as a post-processing step, we erode and dilate the segmentation consequently with a sphere structure with a radius of 2 to remove the noise. Subsequently, we select the largest component in the segmentation map, using connected component analysis.

3 Experimental Results

We work with 100 data samples split 5:1 forming the training and validation set. We validate our approach by comparing the constructed implants to the ground truth, using the Dice score and the Hausdorff distance. The validation results are presented in Table 1. **We experimented with two variations of our**

Table 1. Our score on the validation dataset

Method	Dice	HD-distance
Ours (Transposed Conv)	0.8363	10.6570
Ours (NN upsampling)	**0.9358**	**7.6100**

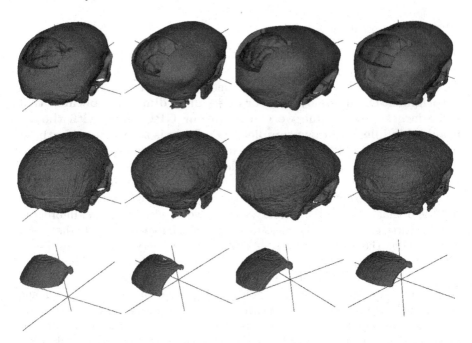

Fig. 3. Qualitative results: The first row depicts four rendered 3D volume of defective scan from the test dataset. The second row shows the reconstructed skull by our method of the corresponding defective skull. The third row is the corresponding cranial implant predicted by our method. We observe that our method generalizes well and accurately reconstruct the skull to predict the cranial implants.

2D decoder model. In the first case, we trained the original decoder, and in the second case, we replace the NN upsampling layers of the 2D decoder with transposed convolution layers. We observe that the 2D decoder with NN upsampling layers performs significantly better than the decoder with transposed-convolution layers. We attribute this to the over parameterization during the upsampling step. Since the image is binary in nature, the nearest neighborhood upsampling layer is sufficient for this task.

Table 2. Our score on the 100 test cases.

Method	Dice	HD-distance
Baseline [12]	0.8555	5.1825
Ours (NN upsampling)	**0.8957**	**4.6019**

Finally, we tested our model on the challenge test set and report the results for cases 000–099 in Table 2. Our model outperforms the baseline method proposed in [12] both in the Dice score and Hausdorff distance. We did not report the results on cases 100–109, since the location of the defect is very different from the training set, and the model could not predict the implant. Figure 3 shows the qualitative results of randomly selected scans from the test data set. Visual inspection also confirms that our model estimates accurate cranial implants for these cases. The source code of our model is accessible from https://github.com/mlentwicklung/autoimplant.

4 Conclusion

We provide an efficient and compact solution for the AutoImplant 2020 challenge, which is suitable for fast and easy deployment. Our key innovation is the incorporation of a two-stage reconstruction policy, where the first stage predicts a coarse-scale implant, and the second stage super-resolve it to a high-resolution one. We achieve accurate implant prediction on the validation dataset. Our model is end-to-end in the high-resolution space and thus can serve as a baseline for developing more complex models aiming to better learn the anatomically invariant implant prediction.

Acknowledgement. Amirhossein Bayat is supported by the European Research Council (ERC) under the European Union's 'Horizon 2020' research & innovation programme (GA637164–iBack–ERC–2014–STG). Suprosanna Shit is supported by the Translational Brain Imaging Training Network (TRABIT) under the European Union's 'Horizon 2020' research & innovation program (Grant agreement ID: 765148).

References

1. Angelo, L., Di Stefano, P., Governi, L., Marzola, A., Volpe, Y.: A robust and automatic method for the best symmetry plane detection of craniofacial skeletons. Symmetry **11**(02), 245 (2019)
2. Bayat, A., et al.: Inferring the 3D standing spine posture from 2D radiographs. arXiv preprint arXiv:2007.06612 (2020)
3. Bhowmik, A., Shit, S., Seelamantula, C.S.: Training-free, single-image super-resolution using a dynamic convolutional network. IEEE Signal Process. Lett. **25**(1), 85–89 (2017)
4. Chen, X., Xu, L., Li, X., Egger, J.: Computer-aided implant design for the restoration of cranial defects. Sci. Rep. **7**, 1–10 (2017)
5. Dai, A., Qi, C.R., Nießner, M.: Shape completion using 3D-encoder-predictor CNNs and shape synthesis. In: 2017 IEEE Conference on Computer Vision and Pattern Recognition (CVPR), pp. 6545–6554 (2016)
6. Egger, J., et al.: Interactive reconstructions of cranial 3D implants under MeVis-LAB as an alternative to commercial planning software. PLoS ONE **12**, 20 (2017)
7. Ezhov, I., et al.: Real-time Bayesian personalization via a learnable brain tumor growth model. arXiv preprint arXiv:2009.04240 (2020)
8. Gall, M., Li, X., Chen, X., Schmalstieg, D., Egger, J.: Computer-aided planning and reconstruction of cranial 3D implants. In: Annual International Conference of the IEEE Engineering in Medicine and Biology Society (EMBC), pp. 1179–1183, August 2016

9. Han, X., Li, Z., Huang, H., Kalogerakis, E., Yu, Y.: High-resolution shape completion using deep neural networks for global structure and local geometry inference. In: 2017 IEEE International Conference on Computer Vision (ICCV), pp. 85–93 (2017)

10. Hu, X., et al.: Feedback graph attention convolutional network for medical image enhancement. arXiv preprint arXiv:2006.13863 (2020)

11. Husseini, M., Sekuboyina, A., Bayat, A., Menze, B.H., Loeffler, M., Kirschke, J.S.: Conditioned variational auto-encoder for detecting osteoporotic vertebral fractures. In: Cai, Y., Wang, L., Audette, M., Zheng, G., Li, S. (eds.) CSI 2019. LNCS, vol. 11963, pp. 29–38. Springer, Cham (2020). https://doi.org/10.1007/978-3-030-39752-4_3

12. Li, J., Pepe, A., Gsaxner, C., von Campe, G., Egger, J.: A baseline approach for Autoimplant: the MICCAI 2020 cranial implant design challenge. arXiv preprint arXiv:2006.12449 (2020)

13. Li, J., Pepe, A., Gsaxner, C., Egger, J.: An online platform for automatic skull defect restoration and cranial implant design. arXiv:2006.00980 (2020)

14. Marzola, A., Governi, L., Genitori, L., Mussa, F., Volpe, Y., Furferi, R.: A semi-automatic hybrid approach for defective skulls reconstruction. Comput.-Aided Des. Appl. **17**, 190–204 (2019)

15. Morais, A., Egger, J., Alves, V.: Automated computer-aided design of cranial implants using a deep volumetric convolutional denoising autoencoder, pp. 151–160, April 2019

16. Navarro, F., et al.: Shape-aware complementary-task learning for multi-organ segmentation. In: Suk, H.-I., Liu, M., Yan, P., Lian, C. (eds.) MLMI 2019. LNCS, vol. 11861, pp. 620–627. Springer, Cham (2019). https://doi.org/10.1007/978-3-030-32692-0_71

17. Sarmad, M., Lee, H.J., Kim, Y.M.: RL-GAN-Net: a reinforcement learning agent controlled GAN network for real-time point cloud shape completion. In: 2019 IEEE/CVF Conference on Computer Vision and Pattern Recognition (CVPR), pp. 5891–5900 (2019)

18. Sekuboyina, A., et al.: Verse: a vertebrae labelling and segmentation benchmark. arXiv preprint arXiv:2001.09193 (2020)

19. Stutz, D., Geiger, A.: Learning 3D shape completion under weak supervision. Int. J. Comput. Vis. 1–20 (2018)

20. Sung, M., Kim, V.G., Angst, R., Guibas, L.J.: Data-driven structural priors for shape completion. ACM Trans. Graph. **34**, 175:1–175:11 (2015)

Cranial Implant Design Using a Deep Learning Method with Anatomical Regularization

Bomin Wang[1(✉)], Zhi Liu[1], Yujun Li[1], Xiaoyan Xiao[2], Ranran Zhang[1], Yankun Cao[1], Lizhen Cui[3], and Pengfei Zhang[4]

[1] School of Information Science and Engineering, Shandong University, Qingdao, China
201712354@mail.sdu.edu.cn
[2] Department of Nephrology, Qilu Hospital of Shandong University, Jinan, China
[3] Joint SDU-NTU Centre for Artificial Intelligence Research (C-FAIR), Shandong University, Jinan, China
clz@sdu.edu.cn
[4] Department of Cardiology, Qilu Hospital, Cheeloo College of Medicine, Shandong University, Jinan, China

Abstract. Cranioplasty is a surgical operation on the repairing of cranial defects caused by the previous operation, ischemic, or hemorrhagic disease, or even after the removal of cranial tumors. It can be performed by filling the defective area with a range of materials. Interactive and semi-automatic computer-aided design tools for cranial implant design are time-consuming and costly. In this paper, we proposed a deep learning method for automatic cranial implant generation. The proposed method mainly included two steps. First, a variational auto-encoder model was trained to learn the latent distribution of complete skulls. Then, the encoder part of the pre-trained VAE together with an encoder-decoder network was trained to generate the complete skull. We design an anatomical regularization term to drive the predicted skull to be more anatomically plausible compared with the ground truth skull. We evaluated the performance of our method using the skull data from the AutoImplant Challenge. The results show that the proposed framework performs well on the 100 test cases while has poor performance on the 10 test cases.

Keywords: Cranial implant design · Convolutional neural networks · Shape completion · Variational Auto-encoder

1 Introduction

Cranioplasty is the surgical repair of a bone defect in the skull resulting from a previous operation, ischemic, or hemorrhagic disease, or even after the removal of cranial tumors, which is a well-known procedure in modern neurosurgery. Cranioplasty can restore the contour and shape of the skull, using either skull subparts from the original complete skull or synthetic bone substitutes with liquid form. Besides, titanium materials and solid biomaterial can also be used as cranial implants. It is challenging to design a cranial implant given the corresponding defective skull. For some situations, the procedure of

© Springer Nature Switzerland AG 2020
J. Li and J. Egger (Eds.): AutoImplant 2020, LNCS 12439, pp. 85–93, 2020.
https://doi.org/10.1007/978-3-030-64327-0_10

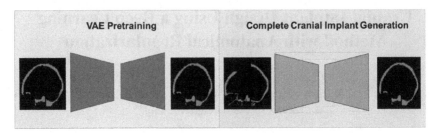

Fig. 1. The workflow of the proposed method.

generating a cranial implant is an ill-posed problem, i.e., there exists an infinite number of solutions, and the implant must fit the skull defect as precisely as possible. Designing the cranial implant is usually performed by professional surgeons on commercial software, which is costly and laborious. Thus, there is an urgent need for a fully automatic and low-cost cranial implant design workflow. In recent years, some interactive and semi-automatic computer-aided design (CAD) tools have been developed. In [1], authors designed a software prototype and workflow including an interactive planning as well as the prediction of cranial implants under MeVisLab. [2] presented a new semi-automatic hybrid approach to reconstruct cranial implants which was landmark independent and avoiding any patch adaptation. However, these methods are still time-consuming and involve human intervention. Cranial implant reconstruction indeed is a volumetric shape completion problem. The AutoImplant Challenge [3] provides a platform to evaluate state-of-the-art methods for the prediction of cranial implants by providing defective skulls with ground truth implant labels.

The main concern of cranial implant generation is whether the predicted implant precisely fit the anatomical shape of the complete skull. However, previous deep learning models cannot provide explicit anatomical constraints. In this paper, we propose a deep learning framework for the automatic generation of an anatomically plausible cranial implant. A variational auto-encoder (VAE) model is first trained on the complete skulls. Then, a U-net based network together with the encoder of the VAE model is used to directly predict the complete skull given the defective skull. We design an anatomical regularization term to drive the predicted skull to be more anatomically plausible compared with the ground truth skull. The final cranial implant can be obtained by subtracting the defective skull from the predicted complete skull. The workflow of the proposed method is shown in Fig. 1.

2   Related Work

With the development of deep learning in the 3D domain, many CNN based methods have been adopted to solve the shape completion problem [4–7]. Volumetric shape completion is a voxel-wise prediction task and thus can be solved by convolutional neural networks used for 3D medical image segmentation. In previous work, encoder-decoder based architectures have been investigated a lot in medical image segmentation tasks. The encoder-decoder model is mainly composed of an encoding path and a decoding path. The encoding path was used to extract image features while the decoding path was responsible to recover dense outputs. Fully convolutional network (FCN) [7] was a typical encoder-decoder based architecture, which has made great progress in medical image segmentation. U-Net [8] included a skip connection between the encoding and decoding paths to fuse high-level and low-level information effectively.

Auto-encoder is a neural network designed to learn an identity function in an unsupervised way to reconstruct the original input. The encoder network in auto-encoder translates the original high-dimension input into the latent low-dimensional code. Different from vanilla auto-encoder, variational auto-encoder (VAE) [9] aimed at mapping data into a distribution. In this way, VAE can generate high dimensional structured data by sampling random code from the learned distribution. In previous work, VAE has been used in various tasks in computer vision, such as image translation, image segmentation, image super-resolution, novel view synthesis, etc. [11–13]. In [13], a pretrained VAE model was used pre-trained to encode complete shape and then was applied to multimodal shape completion in point clouds.

3 Methodology

Inspired by recent work, we propose to combine encoder-decoder architecture with VAE for cranial implant reconstruction. Specifically, we first pretrain a VAE model to learn the latent distribution of the complete skull. Then, we incorporate the encoder part of VAE with an encoder-decoder network to predict the complete skull. The cranial implant can be obtained by subtracting the input defective skull from the output complete skull. The motivation behind the method is that the VAE encoder can map the shape and anatomical structures of complete skulls into compact feature representation and thus we can utilize the VAE encoder in an additional regularization term to guide the encoder-decoder network to produce anatomically plausible skulls. In summary, our method mainly includes two steps, i.e., VAE pretraining and complete skull generation.

3.1 VAE Pretraining

We train a VAE model on the complete skull data from the training set of AutoImplant Challenge. Given a complete skull cx, the encoder part of the VAE model outputs the parameters of a Gaussian probability $q_\theta(z|x)$, where z is a latent vector and θ is the learnable parameters of the encoder. A latent variable z is sampled from $q_\theta(z|x)$ which is further fed to the decoder to reconstruct the complete skull x. The decoder is parameterized by φ. We denote the decoder as $p_\varphi(x|z)$. The objective function is shown as follows:

$$L_{VAE}(\theta, \varphi) = -\mathbb{E}_{z \sim q_\theta(z|x)} \log p_\varphi(x|z) + D_{KL}(q_\theta(z|x) || p(z)) \qquad (1)$$

3.2 Complete Skull Generation

Complete skull generation can be seen as a volumetric shape completion task which is a voxel-wise problem. Volumetric shape completion can be achieved using general 3D

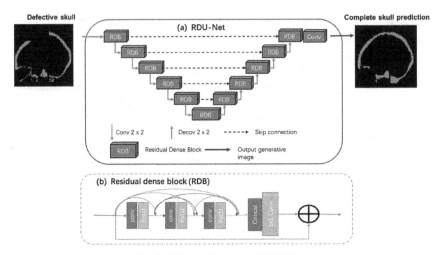

Fig. 2. The architecture of RDU-Net.

encoder-decoder networks that have been adopted in medical image segmentation tasks. In our work, we used a U-Net based model Residual Dense U-net (RDU-Net) to generate the complete skull given the corresponding detective skull. RDU-Net was proposed in [14] which can improve the super-resolution performance of U-Net for accelerated MRI acquisition. The RDU-Net integrated residual dense blocks (RDB) with vanilla U-Net to leverage the power of residual learning strategy and dense feature fusion. The RDBs can make full use of all the hierarchical features and thus enhance the feature expressiveness. We adopt dice loss as an objective function to train the U-Net. The dice loss measures the shape similarity between a defective skull and its corresponding complete skull. To provide anatomically plausible skulls, we add a regularization term to the original dice loss. We incorporate the encoder part of pretrained VAE into the U-Net, which takes the predicted complete skull as input and output two parameters μ and σ, where μ and σ are the mean and standard deviation a Gaussian probability. The dice loss is defined as

$$L_{dice} = \frac{2 * \sum p_{true} * p_{pred}}{\sum p_{true}^2 + \sum p_{pred}^2 + \varepsilon} \tag{2}$$

where p_{true} and p_{pred} are the ground truth complete skull and the output prediction, respectively. ϵ is a small constant to avoid zero division. The regularization term measures the distance between the latent variable of the ground truth complete skull and the output prediction.

$$L_r = \left\| z_{ture} - z_{pred} \right\|$$
$$= \left\| f_\theta(p_{true}) - f_\theta(p_{pred}) \right\| \tag{3}$$

Where z_{ture} and z_{pred} are the latent variables of the ground truth complete skull and the output prediction, respectively. $f_\theta(*)$ is the pretrained encoder of the VAE model.

Hence, the total loss for complete skull generation is

$$L = L_{dice} + \gamma L_r \tag{4}$$

where L_{dice} is a soft dice loss and L_r is the regularization term. γ is a hyper-parameter to control the weight of L_r. We set γ to 0.1 in our experiments. After generating the complete skull, the cranial implant can be obtained by subtracting the defective skull from the complete skull.

3.3 Implementation Details

The encoder of the VAE model consists of four 3D convolution layers with stride 2 and the decoder has the same structure with the encoder except for the up-sampling layers that increase the dimensions of features. We use batch normalization and ReLu for normalization and activation layers, respectively. The convolution kernel size is set to 3. For the RDU-Net model, six RDBs with down-sampling convolution layers are used for generating skull features (the step size of each down-sampling convolution is 2), six groups of deconvolution + RDB are used for up-sampling the features. We set the channel numbers in RDBs to 32. The detailed structure of RDU-Net is shown in Fig. 2. Following the configuration of the baseline method [15], we trained the VAE model and RDU-Net on downsampled defective skulls with resolution $128 \times 128 \times 64$. The predicted implants were upsampled to its original dimension $512 \times 512 \times Z$, where Z is the number of axial slices.

4 Experiments

4.1 Datasets and Experimental Setups

We validated the proposed method on skull data from AutoImplant Challenge. We used all complete skulls from the training set to pretrain the VAE model. The training set then was randomly divided into training data and validation data. The training data included 90 subjects while the validation data consisted of 10 subjects. The RDU-Net was trained on the training data and validated on the validation data. The model with the highest validation performance was selected for testing. We implemented the proposed method using Pytorch (Version 1.4.0) deep learning framework. The learning rate for training RDU-Net was set to 0.0001 and the epochs were set to 400. The experiments were conducted on three NVIDIA RTX 2080Ti GPUs. We did not use any data augmentation during training and no additional defects were created from the healthy skulls in the training set.

4.2 Results

In this subsection, we report the cranial implant generation performance of the proposed method on both the validation set and 100 test cases. The quantitative metrics used for evaluation include the Dice similarity score (DSC) and the symmetric Hausdorff distance. We compared our proposed method with two baseline methods i.e., U-Net and RDU-Net, on the validation set. The quantitative results are shown in Table 1. We can see that with the help of residual dense blocks, RDU-Net outperforms U-Net by 0.0238 and 0.5408 for DSC and HD, respectively. The proposed method performs significantly

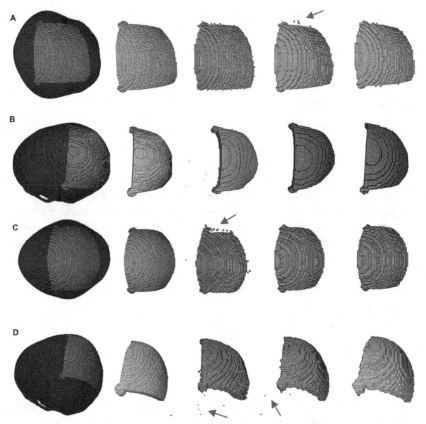

Fig. 3. (A)–(D) qualitative implant prediction results on four cases of the validation set. From left to right: the defective skull with ground truth implant; the ground truth implant; the implant predictions of U-Net; the implant predictions of RDU-Net; the implant predictions of the proposed method. Inaccurate outlier prediction can be seen from the results of U-Net and RDU-Net (red arrows), while our proposed method generated high-quality implants with anatomical consistency. (Color figure online)

better than RDU-Net, which validates the effectiveness of the proposed shape regularizer using a pretrained VAE encoder. We trained the VAE model for 500 epochs, and the DSC of the VAE for complete skull reconstruction can achieve 0.9981 on complete skulls from the training set. We also provide qualitative results of U-Net, RDU-Net, and the proposed method in Fig. 3. Finally, we evaluate our method on the 100 test cases and 10 additional test cases. We had two submissions for the AutoImplant Challenge. The first submission was produced by RDU-Net while the second method was associated with the proposed method. We also compare our method with the baseline method proposed in [15]. The quantitative results are shown in Table 2. The proposed method outperforms RDU-Net both in the DSC and HD, and perform significantly better than the baseline in terms of DSC. However, the performance of our method on 10 additional test cases is relatively poor, since the defect shape and position of the 10 cases are different from the training

Table 1. Quantitative results of the proposed method, RDU-Net, and U-Net on the validation set.

		Validation set (10)
U-Net	Mean DSC	0.8547
	Mean HD	6.4531
RDU-Net	Mean DSC	0.8785
	Mean HD	5.9123
Proposed	Mean DSC	0.8967
	Mean HD	5.2887

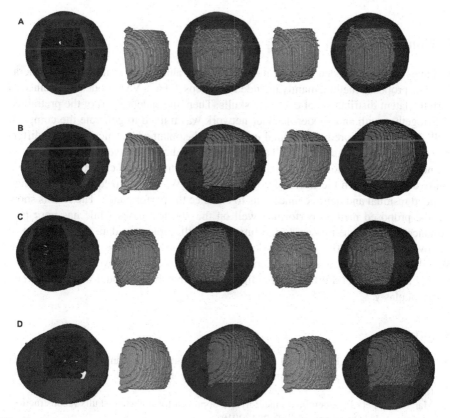

Fig. 4. (A)–(D) qualitative implant prediction results on four cases of the test set. From left to right: the defective skull; the predictions of RDU-Net; the defective skull with the predicted implant of RDU-Net; the predictions of the proposed method; the defective skull with the predicted implant of the proposed method.

set. Figure 4 shows the qualitative results of RDU-Net and the proposed method on the test set.

Table 2. Quantitative results of the proposed method, RDU-Net, and the Baseline method on the test set. The results of the Baseline method on the additional 10 test cases were not available.

		Test case (100)	Test case (10)	Overall (110)
Baseline	Mean DSC	0.8555		
	Mean HD	5.1825		
RDU-Net	Mean DSC	0.8874	0.3510	0.8386
	Mean HD	7.0171	29.4761	9.0588
Proposed	Mean DSC	0.8910	0.4729	0.8530
	Mean HD	6.9091	21.0492	8.1946

5 Conclusion

We have introduced a deep learning method for fully automatic cranial implant generation. The proposed method mainly included two steps. First, a VAE model was trained to learn the latent distribution of complete skulls. Then, the encoder part of the pretrained VAE together with an encoder-decoder network was trained to generate the complete skull. After that, the predicted cranial implant can be obtained by calculating the difference of the generated complete skull and the corresponding defective skull. The intuition behind this is that anatomical regularization can help to produce cranial implants that highly consistent with the shape of complete skulls. We also utilized RDU-Net which included residual and dense connections to enhance the performance. The results show that the proposed method performed well on the 100 test cases while has poor performance on the 10 test cases. In the future, we will implement data augmentation to improve the generalization ability on skulls with various defect shape, size, and position. We will try to incorporate shape constraints in an end-to-end framework instead of pretraining a VAE model. Furthermore, a lightweight CNN based model will be designed for cranioplasty.

References

1. Egger, J., Gall, M., Tax, A., et al.: Interactive reconstructions of cranial 3D implants under MeVisLab as an alternative to commercial planning software. PLoS One **12**(3), e0172694 (2017)
2. Marzola, A., et al.: A semi-automatic hybrid approach for defective skulls reconstruction. Comput.-aided Des. Appl. **17**, 190–204 (2019)
3. Egger, J., et al.: Towards the automatization of cranial implant design in cranioplasty. Zenodo (2020). http://doi.org/10.5281/zenodo.3715953
4. Han, X., Li, Z., Huang, H., Kalogerakis, E., Yu, Y.: High-resolution shape completion using deep neural networks for global structure and local geometry inference. In: 2017 IEEE International Conference on Computer Vision (ICCV), pp. 85–93 (2017)
5. Sarmad, M., Lee, H.J., Kim, Y.M.: RL-GAN-Net: a reinforcement learning agent controlled GAN network for real-time point cloud shape completion. In: 2019 IEEE/CVF Conference on Computer Vision and Pattern Recognition (CVPR), pp. 5891–5900 (2019)

6. Dai, A., Qi, C.R., Nießner, M.: Shape completion using 3D-encoder-predictor CNNs and shape synthesis. In: 2017 IEEE Conference on Computer Vision and Pattern Recognition (CVPR), pp. 6545–6554 (2016)

7. Stutz, D., Geiger, A.: Learning 3D shape completion under weak supervision. arXiv:1805.07290 (2018)

8. Long, J., Shelhamer, E., Darrell, T.: Fully convolutional networks for semantic segmentation. In: IEEE Conference on Computer Vision and Pattern Recognition (CVPR), pp. 3431–3440, Boston (2015)

9. Ronneberger, O., Fischer, P., Brox, T.: U-Net: convolutional networks for biomedical image segmentation. In: Navab, N., Hornegger, J., Wells, W., Frangi, A. (eds.) Medical Image Computing and Computer-Assisted Intervention – MICCAI 2015 (2015)

10. Kingma, D.P., Welling, M.: Auto-Encoding Variational Bayes (2014)

11. Myronenko, A.: 3D MRI brain tumor segmentation using autoencoder regularization. In: Crimi, A., Bakas, S., Kuijf, H., Keyvan, F., Reyes, M., van Walsum, T. (eds.) BrainLes 2018. LNCS, vol. 11384, pp. 311–320. Springer, Cham (2019). https://doi.org/10.1007/978-3-030-11726-9_28

12. Gatopoulos, I., Stol, M., Tomczak, J.M.: Super-resolution variational auto-encoders. arXiv:2007.10618 (2020)

13. Grbacea, C., Oord, A.V.D., Li, Y., et al.: Low bit-rate speech coding with VQ-VAE and a WaveNet decoder. In: IEEE International Conference on Acoustics, Speech and Signal Processing (ICASSP) (2019)

14. Wu, R., Chen, X., Zhuang, Y., Chen, B.: Multimodal shape completion via conditional generative adversarial networks. arXiv:2003.07717 (2020)

15. Kevin Ding, P.L., Li, Z., Zhou, Y., Li, B.: Deep residual dense U-Net for resolution enhancement in accelerated MRI acquisition. arXiv:2003.07717 (2020)

16. Li, J., Pepe, A., Gsaxner, C., von Campe, G., Egger, J.: A baseline approach for AutoImplant: the MICCAI 2020 cranial implant design challenge. arXiv preprint arXiv:2006.12449 (2020)

High-Resolution Cranial Implant Prediction via Patch-Wise Training

Yuan Jin[1,2], Jianning Li[1,2], and Jan Egger[1,2,3](✉)

[1] Institute of Computer Graphics and Vision, Graz University of Technology,
Graz, Austria
egger@icg.tugraz.at
[2] Computer Algorithms for Medicine Laboratory (Café-Lab), Graz, Austria
[3] Department of Oral and Maxillofacial Surgery, Medical University of Graz,
Graz, Austria

Abstract. In this study, we proposed two methods for AutoImplant (https://autoimplant.grand-challenge.org/) - the cranial implant design challenge. The shape of the implant is predicted based on the inputted defective skull. This task can be accomplished either by directly predicting the implant with the defective skull, or indirectly rebuilding the complete skull and then taking the difference between the defective and complete skulls. In our work, a deep learning model is applied to automatically predict the implant. In order to solve the problem that high resolution images can often not be directly inputted to the deep learning model, two proposed methods of resize and patch-based are examined. On the test set, the proposed resize method achieves an average dice similarity score (DSC) of 0.7350 and a Hausdorff distance (HD) of 7.2425 mm, while the proposed patch-based method achieves an average DSC of 0.8887 and a HD of 5.5339 mm.

Keywords: Shape completion · Super-resolution · Cranioplasty · Deep learning · AutoImplant

1 Introduction

A cranial defect usually occurs after injury, tumor invasion or infection. The current process of cranial implant design and manufacturing usually involves costly commercial software and highly-trained professional users [1]. An automatic, low-cost design and manufacturing of cranial implants can bring significant benefits and improvements to the current clinical workflow for cranioplasty [11].

The AutoImplant Challenge [9] is organized in order to tackle the problem of automatic cranial implant design in a data-driven manner, without relying explicitly on geometric shape priors of human skulls [10]. The organizers provide 3D binary images of defective skulls, complete skulls and implants as the datasets, with which the reconstruction of implants can be proceeded either

© Springer Nature Switzerland AG 2020
J. Li and J. Egger (Eds.): AutoImplant 2020, LNCS 12439, pp. 94–103, 2020.
https://doi.org/10.1007/978-3-030-64327-0_11

directly from defective skulls, or from the differences between defective and complete skulls.

As one of the most commonly used approaches, Deep neural networks (DNNs) have achieved state-of-the-art performance in the field of medical imaging [4,5,7,12,13,15]. López-Linares et al. [13] for example, proposed to use 3D convolutional neural networks for abdominal aortic aneurysm segmentation, combining with a data augmentation before the processing in neural networks and a data processing of output images to improve the accuracy. Morais et al. [15] proposed to use an encoder-decoder network to predict a complete skull from a defective skull, which is similar with our work. However, the work of Morais et al. uses skulls with low resolutions (30^3, 60^3 and 120^3) from Magnetic Resonance Imaging (MRI) data, while our work deals with skulls from Computed tomography (CT) data of a higher resolution.

2   Method

This section describes the details of (i) a proposed deep learning model structure for 3D implant prediction, and (ii) two proposed methods for solving the problem that the original skull volumes cannot be directly inputted into a network, in example, because of memory restrictions. This section includes the data description, network architectures, training, and test procedure, proposed resize method, and proposed patch-based method. The evaluation metrics are also described at the end of this section.

2.1   Dataset

The AutoImplant Challenge [9] database comprises 200 binary skull datasets (100 for training and 100 for testing) generated from CQ500 dataset [3]. The dimension of these skulls is $512 \times 512 \times Z$, where Z is the number of axial slices. Each dataset comprises three images: one defective skull, one complete skull and one implant. The implants can be either directly predicted from the defective skulls or indirectly taken from the difference between the complete and defective skulls.

2.2   Network Architecture

The network architecture examined in this study is adapted from the V-Net network architecture proposed by Milletari et al. [14], which is another famous 3D derivation of the U-Net [16]. This model is trained end-to-end on volumes depicting the prostate for volume segmentation. It has shown high performance to deal with 3D imaging problems and has been widely used in the field of medical imaging [2,8,17].

The whole model consists of two paths, which are usually called the compression path and the decompression path. Both of these two paths are divided into different stages for operations with different resolutions.

In the compression path each stage consists of one to three convolutional layers, while in the right decompression path the same stage has similar deconvolutional operations. All the convolutions use volumetric kernels of size $5 \times 5 \times 5$ applied with stride 1 and padding of $2 \times 2 \times 2$ to keep the size of feature map invariant. Between two adjacent stages in the compression path, there is a convolutional operation with $2 \times 2 \times 2$ voxels wide kernels applied with stride 2, which halves the size while double the channels of feature maps in each stage. While in the decompression path a deconvolution operation is employed in each stage concatenated with half the number of convolutional kernels in the same stage of the compression path. This concatenation operation, similar to U-Net, sends the features from the compression path to corresponding positions of the decompression path to reconstruct high-quality images. The prediction is proceeded by the soft-max layer at the end of the V-Net, which outputs the probability of each voxel to belong to the object or not.

Another characteristic of the V-Net is the application of residual learning. Because of the two paths structure, a complete model of V-Net has more than 20 convolutional layers, which strengthen the model to represent more complex features. But more layers can also cause troubles, in which the most important is called the degradation problem. It means with more layers built in a deep learning model, the accuracy rate will saturate first and then decrease sharply. The method of residual learning proposed by He et al. [6] was developed to solve this problem. In this model, the input of each stage is used in following convolutional layers while also added to the output of the last convolutional layer of that stage. This method has handled the problem of degradation well compared with the original U-Net model.

2.3 Resize Method

As shown in Fig. 1, the resize method firstly resizes the original images ($512 \times 512 \times Z$) to a constant size ($256 \times 256 \times 64$). The resized images are inputted directly into the network, of which the outputs are complete skulls. The predicted implants are calculated based on the differences between defective and complete skulls. After that, the implants are resized back to the original resolutions with Gaussian interpolation. Finally a denoising method, which is to keep one object that has the most voxels and remove other objects, is used to improve the prediction accuracy.

The main advantage of the resize method is that all the features of one inputted defective skull can be used simultaneously to predict the complete one, which makes it concise to design and apply the deep networks. Nonetheless, the main problem of the resize method is the accuracy loss during the resize steps. It is crucial to select a suitable method for resizing the implant back to the original resolution.

Original defective skull
512x512xZ

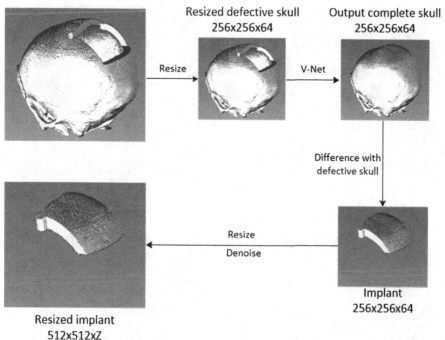

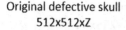

Resized implant
512x512xZ

Fig. 1. Process of the resize method. The original defective skulls are resized to $256 \times 256 \times 64$ and then inputted into the network. The implants are obtained via the difference of the outputted complete skulls and the inputted defective skulls. Finally the implants are resized back to the original sizes and then denoised to improve the prediction accuracy.

2.4 Patch-Based Method

As shown in Fig. 2, the patch-based method splits the original defective skull into 3D slices with a constant size ($256 \times 256 \times 64$). Each slice is a part of the original image and is propagated into the network. The output has the same size of the slice and can be combined to reconstruct the predicted implant. During the reconstruction process, the same denoising method as described in Sect. 2.3 is used.

Compared with the resize method, the patch-based method has some drawbacks, such as the class imbalance and the incoherence between slices. These problems usually occur, because a slice cannot contain all the features from the original image. But these slices can be combined to reconstruct images with original resolutions, so the resize steps, which will reduce the accuracy of the prediction results, are not necessary anymore.

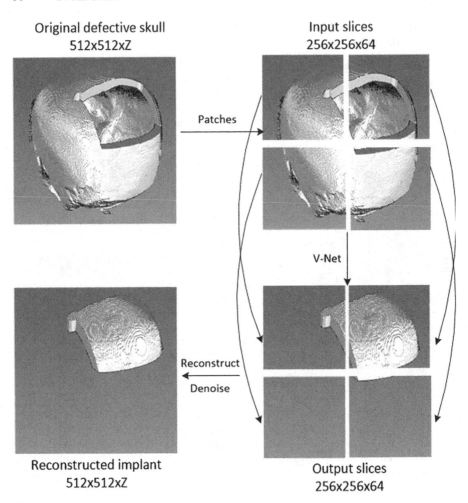

Original defective skull
512x512xZ

Input slices
256x256x64

Patches

V-Net

Reconstruct

Denoise

Reconstructed implant
512x512xZ

Output slices
256x256x64

Fig. 2. Process of the patch-based method. The original defective skulls are split into slices with constant patch shape of $256 \times 256 \times 64$ and stride shape of $128 \times 128 \times 32$. For example, an original image with the size of $512 \times 512 \times 256$ is split into 63 slices ($[0, 256]^2[0, 64], [0, 256]^2[32, 96], [0, 256]^2[64, 128], ...$). All the slices are inputted into the network separately and the resulted slices are combined to reconstruct the implants.

2.5   Evaluation Metrics

Two evaluation metrics, dice similarity score (DSC) and Hausdorff distance (HD), are used in our study to evaluate the results of predicted implants. DSC is a statistic used to measure the similarity of the predicted and ground-truth implants. It is defined as:

$$DSC = \frac{2|P \cap G|}{|P| + |G|} \qquad (1)$$

where $|P|$ and $|G|$ are the number of implants voxels in the prediction and ground-truth images, respectively.

HD is used to measure how far the predicted implants are from the ground-truth ones. It is defined as:

$$d_H(P, G) = \max\{\sup_{p \in P} \inf_{g \in G} d(p, g), \sup_{g \in G} \inf_{p \in P} d(p, g)\} \tag{2}$$

where sup represents the supremum and inf the infimum, and d is the Euclidean distance.

3 Experiments and Results

In this section, we demonstrate the advantage of the proposed resize method and the proposed patch-based method. In Experiment 1, we examine the performance of the proposed resize method on the V-Net model. In Experiment 2, we examine the performance of the proposed patch-based method on the same V-Net model. Both experiments are performed with GPUs from Google Colab (https://colab. research.google.com/). The network is trained for both experiments with a total of 30 epochs. The weights of the network are updated by the Adam algorithm with an initial learning rate $l_0 = 10^{-2}$ following the schedule of $l_0 \times 0.1^{10 epochs}$. For the loss function, a combination of Dice loss and cross entropy loss is used to solve the class imbalance problem of the dataset.

3.1 Experiment 1

In the first experiment, we examined the performance of the proposed resize method on a neural network. We first resized all images of the training and testing datasets to the resolution of $256 \times 256 \times 64$. Thereafter, the model is trained to predict the complete skulls from defective ones. The differences between the input and output are taken to make the implants. We finally resize the implants back to the original resolutions. The experimental results of DSC and HD are shown in Fig. 3 and 4, respectively.

3.2 Experiment 2

In the second experiment, the performance of the proposed patch-based method is examined. We applied the same model structure as for Experiment 1. Slices are created for all datasets with the patch shape of $256 \times 256 \times 64$ and the stride shape of $128 \times 128 \times 32$. In each iteration, one slice is randomly selected to crop the defective skull as input and the implant as ground truth. A limitation is that the model is only trained with patches that have at least one voxel of foreground (implant), in order to reduce the class imbalance problem.

The test data are also cropped into 3D slices with the same shapes of patch and stride as training process. To predict the implants with the original resolutions, all the slices from one original test image are inputted into the network.

The outputs of network are the possibilities of each voxel being the implant. Due to the shape of patch and stride, one voxel can have multiple outputs from the network. The mean value of these possibilities determines the final prediction of this voxel. The experimental results of DSC and HD are shown in Fig. 3 and 4, respectively.

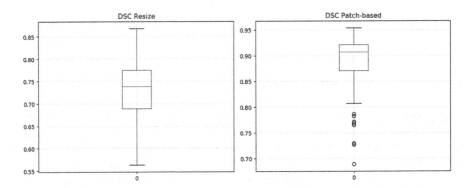

Fig. 3. DSC boxplots of the 100 test cases with resize (left) and patch-based (right) methods.

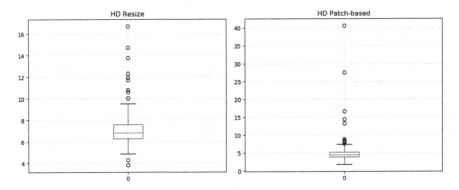

Fig. 4. HD boxplots of the 100 test cases with resize (left) and patch-based (right) methods.

4   Discussion and Conclusion

Due to the computational limitation of training the state-of-the-art networks using GPU, we were not able to input the whole skull volume of size $512 \times 512 \times Z$ to a neural network for training. To overcome this problem, we developed and applied two methods: a resize method and a patch-based method. The former

one changes directly the sizes of the original images and inputs them into the
neural network, while the latter one inputs part of the original images to train
the network.

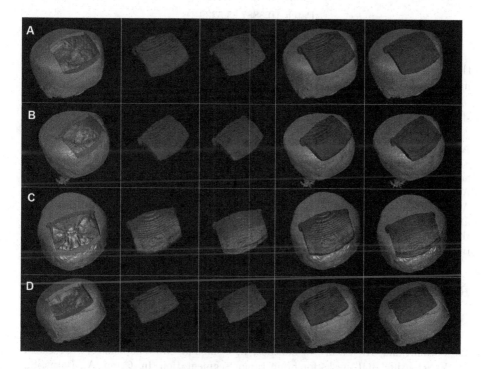

Fig. 5. (A)–(D) implant prediction results on four images from the test dataset. From
left to right: the input defective skulls; the predicted implants with resize method;
the predicted implants with patch-based method; overlay of the implants from resize
method (fourth column) and patch-based method (fifth column) on the defective skulls.
Different colors are used for the implants (red) and skulls (gray). (Color figure online)

Based on the comparison of the testing results in Table 1, even with the
same model structure and training process, the final results with the patch-
based method is much better than the results of the resize method. Hence, it
can be concluded that a simple resize algorithm can lead to big degradation in
the accuracy of images, which is much worse than the problems that occur with
the patch-based method. A qualitative comparison between the results of resize
method and patch based method is shown in Fig. 5.

To improve the resize method, a more accurate image resize algorithm should
be applied to increase the quality of the resized images. As an example, the
original defective skulls can be used as seeds to help with the reconstruction of
the implants with region growing or particle filter algorithms. To improve the
patch-based method, some solutions should be applied to solve the problems
during the training and prediction, such as the incoherence between slices and

Table 1. DSC and HD for the 100 test cases.

	DSC	HD (mm)
Resize	0.7350	7.2425
Patch	0.8887	5.5339

the class imbalance. In our work, during the training process, only slices with implant voxels in ground truth images are used as input, while in the testing process, prediction of one voxel is made based on the combination of all relevant slices.

Acknowledgements. This work was supported by CAMed (COMET K-Project 871132), which is funded by the Austrian Federal Ministry of Transport, Innovation and Technology (BMVIT) and the Austrian Federal Ministry for Digital and Economic Affairs (BMDW) and the Styrian Business Promotion Agency (SFG). Furthermore, the Austrian Science Fund (FWF) KLI 678-B31: "enFaced: Virtual and Augmented Reality Training and Navigation Module for 3D-Printed Facial Defect Reconstructions" and the TU Graz LEAD Project "Mechanics, Modeling and Simulation of Aortic Dissection".

References

1. Digital evolution of cranial surgery. A case study by renishaw plc in new mills, Wotton-under-Edge Gloucestershire, GL12 8JR United Kingdom (2017)
2. Casamitjana, A., Català, M., Sánchez, I., Combalia, M., Vilaplana, V.: Cascaded V-Net using ROI masks for brain tumor segmentation. In: Crimi, A., Bakas, S., Kuijf, H., Menze, B., Reyes, M. (eds.) BrainLes 2017. LNCS, vol. 10670, pp. 381–391. Springer, Cham (2018). https://doi.org/10.1007/978-3-319-75238-9_33
3. Chilamkurthy, S., et al.: Development and validation of deep learning algorithms for detection of critical findings in head CT scans (2018). http://arxiv.org/abs/1803.05854
4. Dai, A., Qi, C., Nießner, M.: Shape completion using 3D-encoder-predictor CNNs and shape synthesis (2016). http://arxiv.org/abs/1612.00101
5. Han, X., Li, Z., Huang, H., Kalogerakis, E., Yu, Y.: High-resolution shape completion using deep neural networks for global structure and local geometry inference (2017). http://arxiv.org/abs/1709.07599
6. He, K., Zhang, X., Ren, S., Sun, J.: Deep residual learning for image recognition. CoRR abs/1512.03385 (2015). http://arxiv.org/abs/1512.03385
7. Hesamian, M., Jia, W., He, X., Kennedy, P.: Deep learning techniques for medical image segmentation: achievements and challenges. J. Digit. Imaging **32**, 582–596 (2019)
8. Lei, Y., et al.: Ultrasound prostate segmentation based on multidirectional deeply supervised v-net. Med. Phys. **46**(7), 3194–3206 (2019)
9. Li, J., Egger, J.: Towards the automatization of cranial implant design for 3D printing (2019). https://doi.org/10.13140/RG.2.2.16144.56324

10. Li, J., Pepe, A., Gsaxner, C., Campe, G., Egger, J.: A baseline approach for AutoImplant: the MICCAI 2020 cranial implant design challenge. In: Syeda-Mahmood, T., et al. (eds.) CLIP/ML-CDS -2020. LNCS, vol. 12445, pp. 75–84. Springer, Cham (2020). https://doi.org/10.1007/978-3-030-60946-7_8. http://arxiv.org/abs/2006.12449
11. Li, J., Pepe, A., Gsaxner, C., Egger, J.: An online platform for automatic skull defect restoration and cranial implant design (2020). http://arxiv.org/abs/2006.00980
12. Long, J., Shelhamer, E., Darrell, T.: Fully convolutional networks for semantic segmentation. CoRR abs/1411.4038 (2014). http://arxiv.org/abs/1411.4038
13. López-Linares, K., et al.: Fully automatic detection and segmentation of abdominal aortic thrombus in post-operative CTA images using deep convolutional neural networks. Med. Image Anal. **46** (2018). https://doi.org/10.1016/j.media.2018.03.010
14. Milletari, F., Navab, N., Ahmadi, S.: V-net: Fully convolutional neural networks for volumetric medical image segmentation. CoRR (2016). http://arxiv.org/abs/1606.04797
15. Morais, A., Egger, J., Alves, V.: Automated computer-aided design of cranial implants using a deep volumetric convolutional denoising autoencoder. In: Rocha, Á., Adeli, H., Reis, L.P., Costanzo, S. (eds.) WorldCIST'19 2019. AISC, vol. 932, pp. 151–160. Springer, Cham (2019). https://doi.org/10.1007/978-3-030-16187-3_15
16. Ronneberger, O., Fischer, P., Brox, T.: U-net: Convolutional networks for biomedical image segmentation. CoRR (2015). http://arxiv.org/abs/1505.04597
17. Tang, H., et al.: Segmentation of anatomical structures in cardiac CTA using multilabel v-net. SPIE Med. Imaging **10574** (2018). https://doi.org/10.1117/12.2293811

Learning Volumetric Shape
Super-Resolution for Cranial Implant
Design

Matthias Eder[1,2] , Jianning Li[1,2] , and Jan Egger[1,2,3(✉)]

[1] Institute of Computer Graphics and Vision, Graz University of Technology, Graz,
Austria
egger@icg.tugraz.at
[2] Computer Algorithms for Medicine Laboratory (Café-Lab), Graz, Austria
[3] Department of Oral and Maxillofacial Surgery, Medical University of Graz, Graz,
Austria

Abstract. Cranioplasty is the process of repairing cranial defects or
deformations, which may be the result of injuries or necessary medical treatments such as brain tumor surgery. For this procedure, it is
necessary to generate a high-quality cranial implant, which needs to be
shaped individually for each skull and each defect. This tends to be a
very time consuming task and requires also in-depth knowledge of various
CAM/CAD programs. In this work, we present a novel automatic three-
stage implant generation pipeline. First, skull completion is conducted in
low resolution using a trained artificial neural network (ANN). Second,
the completed low-resolution skull is sent to a super-resolution network,
which up-samples the low-resolution skull to higher resolution while, at
the same time, filling the skull surface with geometric details. Finally, by
simple subtraction and blob filtering, the desired high-resolution implant
is generated.

Keywords: Shape completion · Super-resolution · Cranioplasty ·
Deep learning

1 Introduction

1.1 Motivation

Cranioplasty is the process of repairing cranial defects or deformations. The
aim of this procedure is to reestablish the aesthetic shape of the head and to
protect the brain from further injuries [2]. To do so, it is necessary to generate
an implant, which has the same size and shape as the original skull fragment.
This has to be done for each patient individually, since each skull can have
unique shape and defect. Currently, the cranial implant design pipeline is built
upon interactive CAD software and involves several steps [1,3,5,9]: acquiring
and segmenting the head CT, converting the skull into 3D model and designing

© Springer Nature Switzerland AG 2020
J. Li and J. Egger (Eds.): AutoImplant 2020, LNCS 12439, pp. 104–113, 2020.
https://doi.org/10.1007/978-3-030-64327-0_12

the implant to fill the defect on the 3D model. Then, the implant is exported to a printable data format (e.g., stl). This turns out to be a time consuming and expensive procedure, which requires knowledge of several different programs and intensive manual work. Given the shortcomings of current clinical practice, Li et al. developed a web-based system that allows a fully automated cranial implant design pipeline [8]. The automated cranial implant design is facilitated by deep learning algorithms [6]. This study aims to explore this possible path and to discover a way to ease cranial implant generation, using deep learning.

1.2   Problem Formulation

The skull reconstruction can be viewed in terms of the simple addition:

$$R = D + I \tag{1}$$

where R denotes the reconstructed skull, D the defective skull and I the cranial implant. This resembles the basic approach of importing the damaged skull into programs like Blender and shaping an implant to fill the hole. A different approach is given by reordering the equation to:

$$I = R - D \tag{2}$$

Here, the implant is generated by subtracting the defective skull from a reconstructed skull. The reconstruction itself can be a fully automated procedure, where the input is D [10]. However, the reconstruction needs to provide the complete skull at a high resolution, which requires large amount of memory. It becomes unfeasible when the available computational resources are limited. To mitigate this problem, we propose a **coarse-to-fine** framework: skull shape completion is first done in low resolution and the resultant coarse skull is then up-sampled to high resolution via a super-resolution network. This framework has the advantage of producing high resolution implant at a low computation cost. The final implant generation is therefore given by:

$$I = f_S(f_R(D_L)) - D \tag{3}$$

where $f_S()$ denotes the super-resolution function, $f_R()$ the reconstruction function and D_L the low resolution representation of the defective skull.

The approach used in the work of Li et al. [4,7] is the most similar to that of this study. In particular, both approaches follow a **coarse-to-fine** scheme in generating high-resolution implants. Li et al. first predict coarse implants from low-resolution data. In the second step, high-resolution (fine) implants are generated based on the coarse implants from the previous step. Each step is based on an autoencoder-style network. Both approaches are fully data-driven and automatic.

2   Methods

2.1   Overview

The aim of this project is to explore a new way for fast and computationally efficient generation of cranial implants. One possible approach for implant generation, using an auto-encoder neural network, has been taken by Morais et al. [10]. This has proven to be a viable way to reconstruct the volumetric shape of a skull, but showed that a high amount of GPU-memory is needed to process any input with a resolution higher than 60^3. To mitigate this problem, this project combines the reconstruction capabilities of convolutional neural network (CNN) with a second network, which is trained for volumetric super-resolution tasks. This is done according to the following steps:

1. First a CNN is trained on low-resolution representation of the defect skulls (30^3) for shape completion.
2. Second, a second CNN is trained for volumetric super-resolution on the output of the first step, which up-samples the low-resolution skull to high resolution. The process is able to recover geometric details on the skull surface compared to using simple interpolation.
3. Third, the cranial implant is generated by subtracting the high-resolution defective skull from the output of the second step.

The advantage of this approach is that the reconstruction can be done at a low resolution and the super-resolution network deals with the high-resolution data only at the last layers, which keeps the memory consumption as low as possible. Figure 1 shows the pipeline.

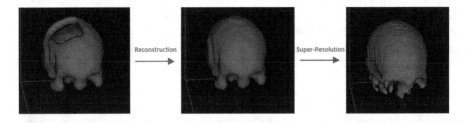

Fig. 1. Skull-Reconstruction Pipeline, including low-resolution skull shape completion and volumetric shape super-resolution. From left to right: low-resolution defective skull and reconstructed skull, high-resolution complete skull.

2.2   Data-Set Preparation

This study is based on the dataset provided by Ana Morais [10]. Three data-sets with resolution 30^3, 60^3 and 120^3 are available. At each resolution, there are 890 training examples, each example consisting of a defect skull and the corresponding complete skull, and 222 test examples. Each skull is formatted as a 3D binary voxel occupancy grid. In this study, the skull shape completion is carried out on resolution 30^3 and the super-resolution network up-sampled the 30^3 skulls to 60^3.

2.3 Skull Reconstruction

Architecture. The structure of the reconstruction network is loosely based on [11]. The idea is that the encoder path of the UNet will be able to learn the shape of the skull and therefore be able to reconstruct the missing parts, while the high-resolution skip connection preserves the existing parts. The chosen structure is illustrated in Fig. 2:

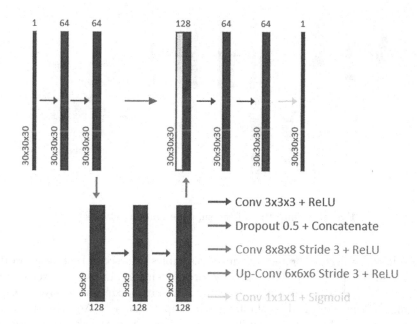

Fig. 2. Architecture of the reconstruction-network. On each layer shows the size of the output as well as the number of feature maps. The kernel size for all the layers is set to 3^3.

Training. The following parameters were chosen to train the network: Training time: 15 epochs. Batch size: 1. Loss-Function: Binary Cross Entropy (BCE). Optimizer: Stochastic Gradient Descent (SGD). Learning Rate: 0.1. Momentum: 0.9. The number of training epochs was chosen relatively small, since plenty of test runs showed a high convergence speed. Training beyond this showed signs of overfitting.

2.4   Skull Super-Resolution

Architecture. The purpose of the super-resolution network is to increase the resolution of the reconstructed skulls (from 30^3 skulls to 60^3). In contrast to a direct up-sampling approach based on interpolation, a neural network learns not only to up-sample a skull but also to recover the geometric details on the skull surface.

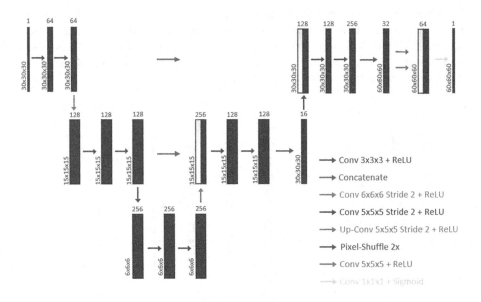

Fig. 3. Architecture of the super-resolution network.

As shown in Fig. 3, the network itself resembles the reconstruction network, as it is also based on the U-Net architecture, but incorporates the pixel-shuffle technique [12] to increase the voxel count. In these pixel-shuffle layers, each resulting channel is formed by shuffling eight input channels. Additional convolutions are used in between to match the channel counts of the skip connections. In the end, a $1 \times 1 \times 1$ convolution is used to reduce the remaining 64 channels to one and a sigmoid layer is used to obtain the final output.

Training. Network training parameters: Training time: 20 epochs. Training-Set size: 890 examples. Validation-Set size: 222 examples. Batch size: 1. Loss-Function: Binary Cross Entropy (BCE). Optimizer: Stochastic Gradient Descent (SGD). Learning Rate: 0.1. Momentum: 0.9.

2.5   Implant Generation

The implant generation pipeline is shown in Fig. 4 and contains four steps: (1) Feed the defective skull (30^3) to the trained reconstruction network. (2) Feed the output of the reconstruction network to the trained super-resolution network. (3) Subtract the high-resolution defective skull (60^3) from the output of the super-resolution network. (4) Filter the output to get rid of noisy voxels.

Fig. 4. Implant generation pipeline.

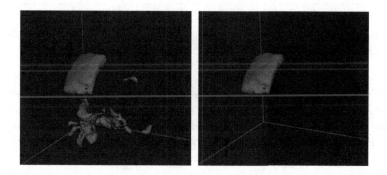

Fig. 5. Implant before and after filtering.

While the super-resolution network preserves the skull shape very well, it tends to hallucinate additional parts in the lower region of the skull. To get rid of these parts and obtain the isolated implant, a 3D connected components analysis was adopted after a morphological "opening" and "closing" operation, which helps to suppress unwanted thin connections among close segments. Since morphological operations degrade the shape and surface of the entire implant, the isolated implant is not used directly but as a segmentation mask on the original unfiltered input. This way the implant is as close as possible to the output of the super-resolution network. Figure 5 shows the effect of such filtering.

3   Results

3.1   Reconstruction

The reconstruction network delivered very good results on the 222 examples of the 30^3 validation data-set. The average dice similarity coefficient (DSC) was

Table 1. DSC of the skull (s) and implant (imp)

	Rec (s)	Super-res (s)	Cubic interp (s)	Super-res (imp)	Cubic interp (imp)
Average	0.9967	0.8128	0.7418	0.8337	0.6883
Min	0.9817	0.6865	0.7069	0.5307	0.4132
Max	1.0	0.8619	0.7639	0.9452	0.7705

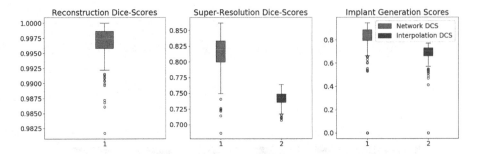

Fig. 6. Dice-Score distribution for reconstruction (left), super-resolution (middle) and implant generation (right)

0.9967 with a minimum of 0.9817 and one perfectly reconstructed example. The DSC distribution is shown in Fig. 6. It is especially noteworthy that the network can reproduce input skull structures perfectly without noticeable hallucination (Fig. 7). Further investigation needs to be taken to figure out whether the network can maintain such high performance on skulls of higher resolution.

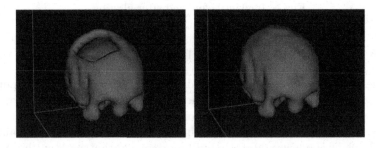

Fig. 7. Sample output of the skull reconstruction network on the 30^3 data.

3.2 Super-Resolution

To rate the super-resolution performance, the up-sampling was also conducted on the skulls by using simple cubic interpolation, which yielded an average DCS of 0.7418. In comparison, the super-resolution network had an average DCS of 0.8128.

As can be seen in Fig. 8, the network output looks substantially more natural than the interpolated version. Still, in comparison with the interpolation, the DSC of the network are distributed with higher variance as can be seen in Fig. 6.

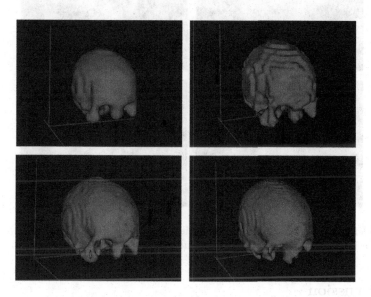

Fig. 8. Low-resolution input (top left), cubic interpolation output (top right), high-resolution target (bottom left), SR-network output (bottom right).

3.3   Full Implant Generation

The final evaluation was carried out on the implants produced according to the pipeline illustrated in Fig. 4. A comparison with cubic interpolation is made. The implants are obtained by taking the difference between the high-resolution defective skulls (60^3) and the corresponding healthy skulls. The healthy skulls come from two sources: interpolation and the super-resolution network. Overall, the network yielded better scores for the implant generation, compared to the cubic interpolation according to Fig. 6. Conducting the implant generation proved more difficult than expected. This is due to the hallucination behaviour of the super-resolution stage. After subtracting the defect skull from the reconstructed skull, these hallucinations lead to blobs, which made additional filtering necessary. The filtering algorithm is very sensitive to thin structures. If these structures remain too big, the filtering concentrates on the wrong parts and thus returns a wrong implant. On the 222 validation examples, this happened 14 times for the network output and 2 times for the interpolation output. By applying opening and closing to the implant, it was possible to fix some of these examples manually. Figure 9 shows a illustration of a implant obtained by interpolation and by the super-resolution network.

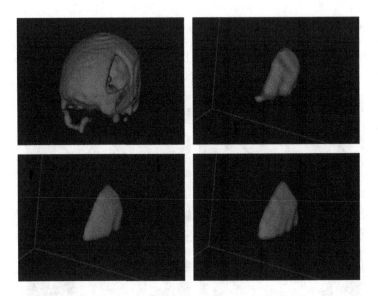

Fig. 9. Defect high-res skull (top left), cubic interpolated implant (top right), super-resolution implant (bottom left), ground truth (bottom right)

4   Discussion

In this project we presented a possible approach to generate implants for cranioplasty. The implant generation was split into 3 parts. Low resolution reconstruction, skull super-resolution and subtraction and filtering. The reconstruction network proved to be a very efficient way to reconstruct the given low resolution data. It provided good scores and high shape accuracy. The super-resolution network also delivered good results compared to an cubic interpolation upsampling stage. While the overall shape of the skull presented itself way more natural, it suffered from random hallucinations introduced by the network. To mitigate this problem more focus needs to be taken on the super-resolution network structure. The high resolution defective skull data could be used in the later layers of the network to act as a guide for the existing skull parts. The suppression of hallucinations turned out to be an important task for the third stage. Here the random hallucination blobs, which remained after subtraction and filtering, lead to problems with the automatic implant generation. Still the network hit higher scores compared to the cubic interpolation variant. In summary, the project showed the potential to create a new and efficient way for automatic cranial implant generation.

Acknowledgment. This work sees the support of CAMed (COMET K-Project 871132), which is funded by the Austrian Federal Ministry of Transport, Innovation and Technology (BMVIT), and the Austrian Federal Ministry for Digital and Economic Affairs (BMDW), and the Styrian Business Promotion Agency (SFG), FWF KLI 678-B31 (enFaced), and the TU Graz Lead Project (Mechanics, Modeling and Simulation of Aortic Dissection).

References

1. Chen, X., Xu, L., Li, X., Egger, J.: Computer-aided implant design for the restoration of cranial defects. Sci. Rep. **7**, 1–10 (2017). https://doi.org/10.1038/s41598-017-04454-6

2. Dujovny, M., Aviles, A., Agner, C., Fernandez, P., Charbel, F.T.: Cranioplasty: cosmetic or therapeutic? Surg. Neurol. **47**(3), 238–241 (1997). https://doi.org/10.1016/S0090-3019(96)00013-4, http://www.sciencedirect.com/science/article/pii/S0090301996000134

3. Egger, J., et al.: Interactive reconstructions of cranial 3D implants under MeVis-Lab as an alternative to commercial planning software. PLoS ONE **12**, 20 (2017). https://doi.org/10.1371/journal.pone.0172694

4. Egger, J., et al.: Towards the automatization of cranial implant design in cranioplasty (2020). https://doi.org/10.5281/zenodo.3715953

5. Gall, M., Li, X., Chen, X., Schmalstieg, D., Egger, J.: Computer-aided planning and reconstruction of cranial 3D implants. In: Annual International Conference of the IEEE Engineering in Medicine and Biology Society (EMBC), pp. 1179–1183 (2016). https://doi.org/10.1109/EMBC.2016.7590915

6. Li, J.: Deep learning for cranial defect reconstruction. Master's thesis, Graz University of Technology, January 2020

7. Li, J., Pepe, A., Gsaxner, C., von Campe, G., Egger, J.: A baseline approach for autoimplant: the MICCAI 2020 cranial implant design challenge. ArXiv abs/2006.12449 (2020)

8. Li, J., Pepe, A., Gsaxner, C., Egger, J.: An online platform for automatic skull defect restoration and cranial implant design. ArXiv abs/2006.00980 (2020)

9. Marzola, A., Governi, L., Genitori, L., Mussa, F., Volpe, Y., Furferi, R.: A semi-automatic hybrid approach for defective skulls reconstruction. Comput.-Aided Des. Appl. **17**, 190–204 (2019). https://doi.org/10.14733/cadaps.2020.190-204

10. Morais, A., Egger, J., Alves, V.: Automated computer-aided design of cranial implants using a deep volumetric convolutional denoising autoencoder. In: Rocha, Á., Adeli, H., Reis, L.P., Costanzo, S. (eds.) New Knowledge in Information Systems and Technologies, pp. 151–160. Springer, Cham (2019). https://doi.org/10.1007/978-3-030-16187-3_15

11. Ronneberger, O., Fischer, P., Brox, T.: U-net: convolutional networks for biomedical image segmentation (2015)

12. Shi, W., et al.: Real-time single image and video super-resolution using an efficient sub-pixel convolutional neural network (2016)

Author Index

Printed in the United States
by Baker & Taylor Publisher Services

Printed in the United States
By Bookmasters